-Intimacy and Depression-

By Ralph H. Desmarais, Ph.D.

Copyright ©1999

All rights reserved

ISBN: 1-58749-195-8

Earthling Press ~ United States of America

Intimacy and Depression by Ralph H. Desmarais, PhD
Copyright 1999

Print edition 2003
ISBN: 1-58749-195-8

Electronic editions 1999
ISBNs: 1-928670-74-1 and 1-928670-75-X
All trade paperback and electronic rights reserved

Printed in the United States of America. No part of this book may be used or reproduced without written permission, except in the case of brief quotations embodied in reviews or articles. For more information address the publisher at www.awe-struck.net.

Published in print by Earthling Press
An Imprint of Awe-Struck E-Books, Inc.
Printed in the United States of America

www.awe-struck.net
www.earthling-press.com

Available in electronic and print formats

Editors Kathryn Struck and Dick Claassen
Cover art by Cathi Stevenson

Author's Note

The conclusions contained in this book are my own. Many of the basic ideas come from interpretations of my own experiences by several different therapists and books that I have read. I am especially indebted to Dr. Bud Hyde for alerting me to the connection between intimacy and depression and for providing many of the key ideas contained herein. His development of the idea of authenticity as distinguished from honesty and the importance of congruently authentic behavior in intimate relationships and depression-free living provided the cognitive basis for my own recovery and the inspiration for this essay.

Table of Contents

Chapter One
Boundaries—Achieving intimacy and maintaining boundaries—the depressed person and boundaries—seeking authenticity and contact

Chapter Two
Isolation and depression—Ways of maintaining isolation—the "perfectionist"—the "alcoholic"—the "workaholic"—the "busy" body- communication that distances—the critic—the advisor—the isolationist body message

Chapter Three
Breaking barriers to intimacy—sadness expressed—anger expressed—learning to give and take—responsive listening—establishing communication

Chapter Four
Moving towards intimacy—authenticity and honesty—feeling with your intimate other—sex and intimacy—maintaining

identities—extending the intimate experience—finding those who are emotionally available

Chapter Five
Intimacy as a cure for depression—ending isolation—curing guilt and low self esteem through authentic communication—resolving anger—taking responsibility

Chapter Six
Living intimately—finding joy in living intimately—building intimacy—setting priorities and maintaining authenticity—ending struggle over control—keeping intimacy alive—shedding the residue of a dysfunctional past

Chapter Seven
Depression and Rebellion—Finding identity and joy through healthy rebellion

Chapter Eight
Depression and Creativity—How the writing profession has used and abused alcohol to cover loneliness and depression and how to avoid these pitfalls

Chapter Nine
Depression and Religion—how organized religion has, at times, fostered sexual repression at the expense of good mental health

Chapter Ten
Depression and the Bureaucrat—how bureaucratic life styles has increased depression and low self esteem by crushing spontaneity

Chapter One

Boundaries and Intimacy

In his widely acclaimed book, *The Road Less Traveled*, Scott Peck describes a common phenomenon; a man in the arms of a prostitute bursts out "I love you" at the moment of orgasm. As soon as the orgasm is over, his boundaries snap back into place and he deals with the prostitute in a business-like manner. For a brief moment he has merged and become intimate; he has lost himself and merged with the prostitute. A good prostitute encourages such merging as it heightens the experience and is good for business. And, to the extent that she is capable of response, she may even feel good about it. In a good relationship, it does not take an orgasm to produce expressions of love. Merging takes place more easily and boundaries are less noticeable. Feelings are expressed and shared; including both the intense and exciting associated with love and sex and the mundane daily fluctuations of temperament common to us all. Hopes and fears, joys and sadnesses, triumphs and defeats are all shared as one.

Still the intimate couple maintain boundaries as separate individuals both with the outside world and with each other. These separate identities are respected and, indeed, encouraged by each. Their different tastes, careers, and political orientation are what they bring into the relationship, and, while subject to discussion, there is no pressure to change. The whole person is loved and accepted.

It is only when differences in style threaten the relationship that decisions have to be made about which is to be given priority—the right to continue the behavior that is causing friction in the relationship has to be weighed against the possibility that the behavior may destroy the relationship. If possible, compromises can be negotiated. A common source of relationship friction is the differences in housekeeping styles of two new mates. Almost every newlywed couple comes up against this problem. It is usually the first major test of the relationship, and it can break the relationship if the couple has not developed a method for resolving conflicts.

If, however, the conflict can be approached as a learning experience, as an opportunity to learn about and respect differences in style and taste, it can bring the couple closer together and promote intimacy. A lot depends upon the manner in which the problem is addressed. If one partner tries to impose his taste on the other and her preferences are not expressed, the stage is set for the festering of hostilities and the creation of anger and depression within the relationship. If one partner feels blamed for not being adequate as an interior decorator, or for not having sufficient skills in household repair, the internalized response will breed anger and depression. That is why it is so essential for the health of the relationship that problems be discussed openly without blame.

In no area is this more crucial than with the sexual life of the couple after the honeymoon wanes and sexual differences become apparent. Sexual appetites are bound to vary and differences in sexual priorities, likes and dislikes will appear. For many, this is the most difficult area of all to openly discuss. For years, women were told by eminent authorities such as Queen Victoria to "lay back and think of England," or some other variation of the submission ritual relating to the rights of husbands and the duties of wives. Women's liberation has brought sexual equality into the bedroom with its goal of love without dependency or possessiveness, but it has not resolved the problem of sexual differences. That remains to be worked out by each couple; each seeking to give and receive sexual gratification, to merge as a couple while retaining their separate sexual identities and balancing and giving equal credence to their different appetites. If one partner starts blaming the other for not meeting their needs without bringing the problem out in the open, or if one never lets the other know what they desire sexually, then the road to anger, frustration and depression is opened.

One key to good relationships is the capacity to be flexible when faced with questions of where the individual's boundaries end and that of the relationship's begin. As the areas of shared experience grow, the relationship should grow accordingly. The boundaries of the relationship tend to grow outward. The relationship changes as the honeymoon period wanes and the couple begin to settle the mundane problems of maintaining a joint household, with all of the financial and other stresses that go with modern life. This can be disturbing for those whose identity is underdeveloped or whose identity boundaries are overly rigid. The danger then is twofold. For those with rigid boundaries, compromising any issue may be seen as threat to personal identity.

On the other hand, difficulties in maintaining one's individual identity can very real when one partner is weak and the other strives to dominate. Sometimes this "feels" normal as, for example when an emotionally immature male seeks a mother figure to take care of him. Or, the obvious reverse, when an immature female seeks a father figure to take care of her. Either way, the potential for growth within the relationship suffers because of the submission of child to parent with the dissolving of adult identity boundaries on the part of the child-partner. The result is a symbiotic relationship that contains the elements for its own ultimate destruction.

Anger and depression will ultimately cloud the relationship as each partner begins to resent the position that they have placed themselves in; the responsibilities of lifelong parenting become burdensome for the dominant partner as does the submissive child position with its implicit denial of self. Neither can be maintained without eventual depression or rebellion affecting the relationship.

With the depressed person, the whole process of developing the relationship while maintaining boundaries becomes fraught with difficulties. Depression usually causes a hardening of the individuals boundaries. It may appear that the depressed person is yielding to demands made upon him or her, but usually the emotional withdrawal accompanying most depressions means that some other process is going on. The apparent yielding to the demands of the mate may be based on a desperate attempt to bond and to escape the pain and loneliness of depression. Since this does not usually achieve the intended purpose, it may encourage the depressed person to give up ever larger chunks of their own identity in order to gain temporary relief from the pain of depression. The ultimate result may be a nervous breakdown, suicide, or attacks upon the mate as anger over the unequal position builds up. The attacks may be passive-aggressive, and mostly unconscious, but none-the-less a cycle has begun that breeds unhealthiness for the relationship.

Each partner brings into the relationship a residue of conditioned reaction based upon his or hers family experiences. The place within the family, the relationship with parents and siblings, the emotional environment established by the dominant family member, all has a bearing on how an individual will respond in a relationship. Responses to these family situations, learned as a child are extremely difficult to overcome.

Some children learn to use withdrawal as a tool to gain enough control over her own emotions to prevent an overpowering parent from completely dominating her. This is a beneficial skill since it allows her to come through a potentially destructive situation with her identity intact. Used in a marriage, it is a powerful tool and may achieve temporary victories, but in the long run it breeds anger and resentment in those who are the target of the withdrawal and will kill the relationship as it never resolves problems in a mutually satisfying way.

Depression is sometimes a more serious form of the withdrawal technique; one partner gets depressed at the other until his or her needs are met. The results are the same, temporary victory at the cost of self-esteem and the ultimate demise of the relationship.

Sometimes the dominant person in the relationship imitates the role played by his dominant parent and will seek to maintain security by controlling most basic relationship decisions—demanding that the house be kept up in accordance with his tastes and that their social life revolve around his world. Sometimes a depressed style of living is learned in the home and carried into other relationships. Usually some treatment for the depression is learned along with it and that too will be carried into other relationships.

If the dominant person has learned to alleviate the effects of his depression through sexual activity, as the alcoholic sometimes seeks to treat depression with ever increasing quantities of alcohol, and the submissive partner yields to his demands in order to maintain the relationship, a co-dependency situation may arise. As long as the addicted person creates the kinds of demands upon the relationship that can only be met by the care taking, self-denying codependent partner the relationship may hang together. But if either partner gets cured, either of the addiction or self esteem problem that goes with co-dependency, then the relationship will fall apart.

Most bad relationships are some kind of codependent match, where the needs of one are seemingly fulfilled by the other—this seems to be true whether the needs are conscious, as with the alcoholics need for alcohol, or unconscious, as with the perfectionists drive to please a long dead parent. People will seek those who seem to fill their needs. During the honeymoon, this mutual need-filling is what may "feel wonderful" and, when the emotional output is high on the part of one partner, it may stimulate the physical or kinesthetic output of the other so that a seemingly perfect match is achieved, but neither all the emotional or all the kinesthetic energy can be sustained if only one of the partners is responsible for all of it. Both will eventually become frustrated and each will begin looking around for some other way to get their needs met.

Styles of depression differ but the result in a relationship is usually the same; anger, isolation and distance become the most obvious features of the relationship. The controlling-dominant-kinesthetic-depressed person like the yielding-submissive-emotional-depressed person both may get some temporary relief from their behavior, but it is at the expense of their relationship. There is no chance for intimacy and the relationship withers. Both maintain emotional boundaries that make them unavailable either to the other or to anyone else.

Traditionally, controlling-depressed people fight the very idea that they are depressed. If they are in control of all other areas of their life, how can it be that their emotions are not within their mastery? Sometimes these are very generous people who give much to the people they dominate; but they withhold themselves. Their boundaries are too rigid to allow the other person to know them in an intimate way. Lacking intimate human contact creates loneliness and depression. By keeping very busy and filling their lives with material interests, they can keep this sadness at bay. But it is always there, ready to seep into their consciousness whenever they are forced to take time to look at their lives.

The submissive person may feel that the depression is part of the contract; she must feel depressed to maintain the relationship, but as with other areas of her life, she must not complain too often or too loudly or the relationship will be engendered. Her conditioning to be a martyr; to look for her rewards in some other life, bring her to the church for solace. But it isn't God that she needs so much as a sense of being valued for her own sake and some genuine love and affection. This may explain why so many ministers and therapists are tempted by their female parishioners and patients and why the rate at which they succumb seems to be on the increase. Although the problem is at least as old as Hawthorne and the *Scarlet Letter*, it is only recently that it has been openly discussed as more and more avenues into the results of depression, sexual addiction and codependency are explored.

Codependency is a variation of passive dependency where the dominant partner is addicted to alcohol, sex, or drugs and the submissive partner learns to use the addiction to maintain the relationship and hence becomes codependent on and may even help maintain the addiction. The symptoms are; excessive care taking, low self-worth, suppression of one's needs and a consequent lack of a sense of identity. The way out of depression is to gain authentic contact with others that will allow them to experiment with relationship building, self-esteem maintenance, and achieving flexibility in utilizing their identity boundaries. That is what the rest of this book is about, the process of working out of isolation towards authentic contact with others; and, particularly, that significant other that one lives with.

Chapter Two describes in more detail the different ways isolationist behavior is manifested—distancing mechanisms that keep other people away. In Three, these barriers are broken down, and, in Four, the movement towards intimacy is started. In Five, intimacy as a cure to depression is examined, finally, in Chapter Six the process of keeping an intimate relationship alive is detailed.

Chapter Two

Keeping Others Away, or...How to Stay Depressed by Avoiding Contact

A recent estimate of the number of people who have had at least one disabling bout with depression places the number somewhere between 10 and 20 million. At any given time, an estimated ten million people are consciously suffering from depression. In addition to these, there are untold millions who have their own sadness and potential depression hidden to themselves if not to the perceptive observer. It is to these people who may or may not have an inkling that something is wrong with there lives—that the joy of living doesn't seem to be there—to whom this section is addressed. To do this, we are first going to indulge in a little stereotyping to illustrate isolation mechanisms that serve both to keep the person who uses them from establishing the kind of contact with others that could bring joy into his or her life. Hopefully, those who find themselves in these categories can work out a strategy with the help of subsequent chapters that will allow them to break out of the patterns of isolation they have established and start enjoying their existence.

The Perfectionist and the Prodigal Son Syndrome:

The "perfectionist" is one of the most common syndromes found in American society. It is a syndrome that afflicts both male and female with some frequency; but, for ease of illustration we have used the male gender in our analysis. Because they are usually successful in the business or profession of their choice, most people see them as objects of envy. They can, indeed, acquire all the outward symbols of success: cars; beautiful women; big houses; the key to the executive washroom. Yet, they have a tiger inside them that won't let them be happy—they can never be quite as perfect as they want. Usually the tiger is the residue of internalized messages that came from a critical mother or father. No matter what they do, it never seems enough to satisfy either the verbalized messages of disapproval from living parents or the internalized messages from long dead parents that the perfectionist keeps persecuting himself with.

His depression results from never achieving the satisfaction with achievement that most others would find more than adequate. Similarly with relationships, no one can meet his expectations. Hence he ends up lonely, a victim of his super critical dealings with both himself and the people around him. His loneliness breeds depression and anger. Since he can't stand criticism, he will not allow anyone to know him, especially, his fears, his weaknesses, his anger and loneliness. His barriers are raised high, and it will usually take a monumental crisis, such as, divorce or getting fired to bring him to seek help. Until that time he maintains his isolation from others by working towards perfection in his work, his attire, his home and his automobile. All this keeps him occupied outward and, until something dramatic happens, he need not heed the sad feelings that sometimes grip him when he awakes in the night. Sleep medication at night and during the day, alcohol, caffeine and other mood elevators help quell the dissatisfaction he feels, but will not address. Or, he may turn towards health perfection, and achieve his lift from natural endorphins, but no matter what he does, it is never enough. He will always look, not at what he has achieved, but at how it could have been done better or faster.

Such behavior isolates him for he never has time for others. He is too busy seeking perfection. Since he is unwilling to share his feelings, even if he has time, his encounters with others are bound to be superficial exchanges with the perfectionist seeking out those who can help towards his goals. All others are brushed aside as being a waste of time. His wife is expected to keep the perfect house and help him in his career. Her feelings about that role and what it does to her self esteem are irrelevant. He will not discuss it, unless she rebels and threatens to leave him.

He needs intimacy to give him a feeling of connectedness and self worth, but refuses to recognize it, and does not have the skills to find it. He may be helped by reading this book, seeking out those who can teach him what he needs to learn, and begin the long process of change. Others may have to await the tragedy that is almost sure to come from a rebellious wife seeking divorce, or from an employer fed up with his eternal criticisms to the point where he is terminated.

As in the biblical story of the prodigal son, the perfectionist is usually the eldest son or daughter of perfectionist parents. They can usually be counted on to follow the provided model closely. Younger sons are not always so compliant. They may rebel by following the example of the prodigal son or some other rebellious pattern which will separate him from the parental model which he rejects. For the rebellious younger son, the road to healthy self-esteem and the capacity for intimacy can be just as blocked as with his perfectionist brother. He may not have internalized the perfectionist messages sent to him by his parents to the extent that his older brother has, and because of this he may have great difficulty finding a set of values that will aid him on his quest for self identity. Rejecting his parents and feeling rejected by them, he is like a lost soul seeking family substitutes for his discarded family structure. The church or the military are filled with these lost souls, and, in fact, the medieval principle of primogeniture which left the family property to the eldest son, provided for the younger ones by finding them positions in the church or military.

In his search for a mate, the younger son may end up searching for a companion who resembles his perfectionist mother that he was never able to please and to seek the love and affection from her that was denied to him as a child. Since the perfectionist mother substitute is usually unable to fill the emptiness that he feels, she too is rejected and the cycle may be repeated endlessly.

His self-esteem battered by parental rejection and an inability to relate to others, he may rebel against all aspects of the society that seem joined to that rejection. Feeling powerless to form successful intimate relationships, he may turn against society as well as parents. Political rebellion may keep him busy enough to ignore, for a time, the sadness he feels because of his isolation, but whenever he slows down, gets sick, or leaves another woman, the sadness overwhelms him as it did with his perfectionist, older brother. Both in different ways are responding to the deficiencies in their family which deprived them of the love, affection, and self-esteem that could have saved them from the compulsive behavior they both indulge in.

The sadness they both eventually feel may be the route to

their salvation, for in seeking help to relieve the sadness, they may find a therapist that can guide them through the maze of their own history to a healthier life style based on authentic responses rather than conditioned reflexes. This book may be of some help if it brings people with similar afflictions to examine their past before they are driven to it to relieve their depression, or before they self-medicate their sadness with alcohol or other drugs.

Alcoholics:

Alcoholics turn to drink for a large number of reasons, many of which are unknown; alcoholism is an extremely complex phenomena. For some, though, alcohol offers an easily obtainable relief from the feelings of isolation and sadness they feel because they have never learned to relate to others on anything other than a superficial level. The alcohol disguises the sadness and deadens the pain for the perfectionist and a lot of others who are depressed for other reasons. That is the reason it is usually safe to assume that it is the alcohol that is sought in bars, not the human companionship. The conversation in most bars is very superficial—work, sports, women or men as sex objects, and gossip are the most frequent topics. The alcohol serves to make what is superficial seem deep and satisfying. But it only does so for the moment—hangover and sadness come together when the alcohol wears off. The alcoholic seeks more to drink to hide the pain, trying to make what is a temporary high for most people into a permanent state. He is doomed to failure. Eventually, he runs out of money and bottoms out and dries out or dies.

Because the booze itself is a barrier to communication, it must be eliminated before any progress can be made towards intimacy. That famous Step One of Alcoholics Anonymous by which the alcoholic admits his powerlessness to control his drinking and turns the problem over to a higher power sets the stage for what is the first breaking of the alcoholics booze barrier and prepares him to relate to something outside himself. Most of the other steps encourage the involvement of the recovering alcoholic with both the group which is supporting his sobriety and those people that have been affected by his drinking. The program itself does not guarantee that intimate transactions shall occur, but the setting provides maximum opportunity for them to do so. The problem with the AA program is that it rarely gets to the heart of what the alcoholic is covering up with his drinking. If the alcoholic stays off booze, that is usually all that is asked. Most usually leave AA without the internal healing that comes with true recovery (this is recognized by AA itself with its references to "recovering Alcoholics", i.e., those that have achieved sobriety but are not cured of whatever was causing them to succumb to addiction). It is relatively rare for the entire twelve steps to be worked and followed with any psychological understanding. AA groups are lay led, and while this does not diminish their effectiveness, it does limit the psychological sophistication of the group. Hence a lot of rote, mechanical reading of the steps goes on without any assurance that the implications behind the steps are understood.

The alcoholic can find the kind of shallow repartee that he used to find in bars in the AA meeting and he can substitute attendance at the meetings for going to bars, which will help him stay sober until he finds some other way to relieve his loneliness. Unfortunately, the twelve steps provide only an introduction to healthy ways to establish human relationships and is basically only a method of maintaining sobriety. The recovering alcoholic frequently becomes a workaholic, a food junky, or a caffeine addict. One only has to attend a few AA meetings to see the evidence of caffeine and nicotine addiction. Sexual addiction and co-dependency are also common, although they are less obvious and require more intensive listening to ascertain.

No one would argue that it is not a wonderful thing for an alcoholic to give up drinking, that is a change for the better for sure, but the recovering alcoholic needs to be trained to find healthy, intimate relationships before he can really say he has gone to the root of his problem and come out without addictions and with an understanding of how to relieve the loneliness and depression that turned him into an addict to begin with. What has been said about the alcoholic also applies to the heavy drinker, since he is only one control level away from alcoholism, and may be drinking for the same reasons. It is true of other forms of addiction even if you stretch the definition of addiction to the limits advocated by Ken Keyes as any emotion-based need.

Much addictive behavior stems from the self treatment of underlying depression—the search for something outside of one's self that will alleviate the internal pain. Alcohol and other drugs dull the pain directly and therefore are the most commonly accepted ways to deal with pain. They are addictive for people who use them on a regular basis for reasons that they are not usually fully aware of. In addition to drugs and alcohol, any intense activity which brings the individual out of himself to avoid his pain will accomplish the same end. Political or religious activity, work, exercise, or sex if done with a consuming vigor will hide underlying depression by providing a high. Sometimes sheer will power combined with the support of sympathetic peers can cure the immediate addiction, but only careful and intensive therapy can reveal and reduce the underlying causes. Only then can the recovering addict change his addictive behavior to that which serves himself rather than treats his depression. He must learn to asses his feelings, articulate them and energize them in an authentic expression of his being rather than one more manipulative attempt to hide his pain and depression from himself. When he is truly authentic, his feelings, thinking and behavior will all be in congruence. What follows is an example from my own experience of how hiding depression with alcohol and compulsive exercise usually will not work for long.

Turned on to Tuna and Horrible Harry: A Dysfunctional Relationship:

It was the Dolphin stories that finally got to me. After all, my kids had been brought up on Flipper and the thought of him caught in a net so that I could have my usual Tuna sandwich for lunch was just too much. My mind revolted and my stomach followed. It had happened to me with veal once before. A picture of those sad looking young heifers all cooped up and never allowed out to play so that their cutlets would be muscle-free had caused a similar mind-stomach response. I never touched veal again. My friend, Horrible Harry, had been responsible for my Tuna lunch. Harry was not horrible all the time—just when he was drunk which, unfortunately was fairly often. When I knew him, Harry and I shared a similar philosophy regarding alcohol; it was to be taken frequently and in as large amounts as were consistent with good health and career advancement. A corollary of this basic philosophy was that extra measures had to be taken to stay in shape if our intake of alcohol was maintained at a sufficiently high level to meet our standards. There were all those extra calories in the beer we drank that had to be worked off, vitamins that had to be taken to replace those drained away by the alcohol, and endorphins summoned to invigorate the mind and body after the nightly abuse to both systems caused by excessive consumption. Diet was important. We both knew this since we both had relatives who were drunks and we had watched them ignore their food needs and try to live on booze alone. We had also seen those who ate and drank grow fat. Hence our concern with nutrition even before it became popular with the general population.

Harry was a Tuna fanatic. He ate a whole six and a half ounce can every day straight out of the can for lunch. He ate it right there in his office while he worked. Washed down with orange juice and black coffee, he claimed it quickly and cheaply met all of his needs as it had met all the fish's needs and he could attend to his career while others were out socializing at lunch. This allowed him to break away early enough for serious beer drinking after our seven mile run. The beer, he claimed, had sufficient carbohydrates, the tuna supplied the protein and the orange juice the vitamins—so with the running to work off the excess calories—we should stay healthy. We both threw in some weightlifting and calisthenics for good measure and, in the summer, we would bike and swim as well.

I kept up with Harry in most of this except for the beer drinking—no one I knew could do that. Harry and I had both been bred and trained for endurance. Harry was a product of the steel towns of Pennsylvania, while I hailed from the textile area of New England. Harry's childhood training had been harder and more brutal than mine. His father had beaten him senseless for withholding cash from his paper route to buy books. He had to educate himself on the sly, stealing both his books and the time to read them from an environment that discouraged personal growth. He learned how to both blend with that environment and still be different from his peers. His great endurance helped him do both.

I had learned some of the same lessons and developed some of the same endurance which is why Harry and I became friends. When I met him, he was finishing up a Ph.D. thesis in English while I was doing one in History. We would drink together and blast the system that made it so easy for some and so hard for guys like us that had to fight for every break we got. We both had married wives that had come up the hard way, too, but they both had had middle class training which made it easier for them to accept their positions in the small college where they taught. Harry and I never felt accepted nor did we accept our newly-acquired status. Hence, we both militantly defended those working class attitudes that we now found were under attack.

Drinking and a life style that had drinking as a primary focus was a given. We never questioned the necessity to drink and never considered spending our free time in any other way. In our families, this is the way it had always been, and, for us we thought it was the way we wanted it to be. So we went to these extraordinary lengths to make it all possible.

And, it seemed to work. Harry got to be chairman of the English Department of the college where I met him and I went on to teach history in Arkansas. Ultimately though, my body faltered. The problem, as I saw it then, came with the switch to vodka. Beer was so expensive in Arkansas relative to Wisconsin where it was almost as cheap as water that I refused to buy it and switched to cheap vodka. But the vodka packed a wallop. Even though I followed Harry's guidelines and mixed it with orange juice, it raised my blood pressure precipitously. In addition, my marriage went to pieces and I lost my job. Motivated at last, I sought help. The doctor I consulted was a recovering alcoholic himself and sniffed out my problem immediately. His prescription was the one that I had been avoiding my entire adult life, "Stop Drinking!"

I listened, stopped and my health improved. I eventually got another job and another wife. My break with the culture of booze loosened the bonds created by my family, and the French-Canadian working class milieu that I had worked so hard to keep intact.

Harry, however, kept the faith. I saw him once after I stopped drinking at a conference in St. Louis. He was in the bar and hailed me over for a beer. I explained to him about my blood pressure, but he was not easily put off. He took my refusal to drink with him as a personal affront and began living up to his name. "Horrible Harry" had never let loose his anger on me before and it wasn't until years later that I realized what his anger was about. I had deserted Harry. I had left him mired in booze and in his working class. Now he was alone for we were a dying breed.

It had become harder and harder for the working class to make up the ladder in academia. The G.I. Bill for the Vietnam vets was not as good as it was for us and when that dried up the ladders down into the lower classes were few and far between. Even the teaching jobs which saw us through graduate school were not there anymore. Harry found himself surrounded by middle class wimps who couldn't or wouldn't drink in the old way.

But even Harry with all his stamina, elaborate diet, and exercise regime could not really afford to down all that alcohol either, but he would die rather than admit it. Such was his commitment to his family and his class. Thankfully, my commitment to life overrode family and class. I hated to leave Harry to his fate because male friends are hard to find and even harder to keep. I guess the shrinks would say it was a dysfunctional relationship because it was based on alcohol. We both came from dysfunctional families and we were both in our own way reliving that dysfunctional syndrome. But we were not merely copying the family history. We both were trying to adapt our backgrounds to a new way of life among books and middle class people.

We had difficulty deciding what we could and could not carry with us into the new life and although Harry and I ultimately parted over booze, he still helped me stay alive. For even after I gave up alcohol, I kept exercising and eating tuna fish (I gradually modified the straight-from-the-can routine to include fruit, vegetables, and rice). Hence, I avoided many of the middle age diseases that took away several of my less attentive peers. I miss Harry and miss the booze. I am happy to be alive and am still searching for that sense of solidarity and comradery that we used to have. I have been told that spiritual communion is possible that is every bit as good as that old, boozy feeling but I am not sure about that. Sometimes on a long bike ride or in an intensive group therapy meeting, I think I have found it, but it slips away, and unlike the booze and Harry, there is no way to duplicate the experience. I guess, all I can do is be ready, sober and receptive whenever the possibility of spiritual communion presents itself.

Workaholics:

The same analysis may be applied to some workaholics and super busy people who use these life styles to avoid feeling the pain of loneliness and depression that comes with the inability to relate to people in an intimate and authentic way. They have erected barriers through which other people dear to them may not be able to break through. They never slow down long enough for them to feel their own pain and don't how to seek the comfort that is available to them from an authentic exchange with others who could relate to them and ease the pain of their loneliness and the depression that goes with it.

Many of the unfortunate types described above, developed the barriers to intimacy after early childhood exchanges with adults who drove them away with inappropriate or even destructive responses to the child's natural inclination to seek love and affection, which is a form of intimacy. Sons and daughters of busy people soon learn to imitate their parents and hide their sad and lonely feelings since the parents have no time or inclination to respond to their needs. They give what they can in a hurry—usually some useless piece of advice, such as; "work hard" "be clean and neat" "save your money." Since this is not the love, affection, or intimacy that the child needs, he learns to swallow his feelings and do "what's right" to please his parents.

If he has a perfectionist parent, he will never please the parent who always can be expected to focus on what is wrong rather than what is right. Hence the child always can expect criticism. Accustomed to criticism, he may seek a perfectionist mate to replace his parents. With a critic for a parent and a critic for a mate, he gets lifelong persecution and the distancing that criticism brings with it rather than the intimacy he really wants. Work becomes something that he can do and from which he can get the kind of acceptance he never got from his parents or wife and hence is motivated to spend most of his time away from family and on the job. While he becomes adept at pleasing his boss, he never pleases himself and may drive every one around him away with his impossible demands. He will not know how to seek love and affection and may not recognize its importance. Like the alcoholic, he is on a death ride that will only end when the stress of continual struggle wears some of his vital organs out. He then may be forced to come to grips with his behavior and, through sheer will. may turn from work to play. But unless he understands what is driving him and is willing to learn the rewards of intimate relationships and end the pain of deprivation that has gripped him, he will merely transfer the drive that impelled him to be a workaholic into the play therapy prescribed by his physician.

Advisors And Other Avoidance Techniques:

Next to criticism, perhaps the most common form of distancing communication we mentioned above was advice. But advisors are not just parents. Barrooms are usually filled with advisors who can solve all manner of problems. They can give advice but can't relate to the feeling behind the problem under discussion for that would reveal their own pain.

Some people don't have to speak at all to let you know that they are not emotionally available. There are academics huddled behind books, music freaks with their ears covered with stereo headsets, athletes forever doing one kind of workout or another. There are people hiding behind layers of fat, people who won't look in your eyes, and people who sit upright and rigid and look at you down their noses. Some people smile all the time to hide their sadness, or cross their legs and arms to ward off entry. Most common is the avoidance of eye contact, or the blank stare, both of which are designed to distance the person that is attempting to make contact. The message is quite clear; "Leave me alone." Most people will respect that message.

Others may hide their detachment and appear outwardly cooperative while carefully hiding their emotions and true feelings. They remain reserved and wait for others to pursue them emotionally. Some may be detached because of anxiety created by the relationship itself. They are anxious about either becoming too close or they are afraid of getting involved and then losing the relationship. The result is painful both for them and those who pursue them as neither can get their needs met in that kind of encounter. It is like a game of chase where one is allowed to get only so close to the target before it is pulled away.

In a recent book on relationships, Harvil Hendrix divided the world between "fusers and isolationists", those desperately seeking someone to fuse with and those wishing to enhance their independence. Much of the stress in marriage can be traced to the continual push and pull exerted by these opposing needs; the fuser pushing for closeness and the isolationist pulling back to preserve independence. As Hendrix sees it, both the fuser and the isolationist are motivated by unresolved needs stemming from childhood experiences; the fuser having been denied affection while the isolationist was kept too close to his overly-protective mother. They both want their relationship to make them whole by filling these opposing needs. A power struggle ensues as each struggles to get the other to conform to their needs. Disappointment, anger and sadness usually are main results of the struggle. The relationship can only be saved if the couple is willing to stop doing battle and begin to recognize and attend to the needs of the other.

As with the fusers and isolationists, all of those described above ultimately must face their own sadness and anger if it is not to ruin their lives. Depression can kill a relationship and even drive a person to suicide if it is allowed to continue unrelieved. The rest of this book offers some help by suggesting ways to break down the barriers to intimacy, how to move towards authentic communication, how to remove some of the causes of depression, and how to maintain intimate relationships. No one should use a book as a substitute for medication or therapy if that is what is needed. The book is meant only as guide and as an aid so that medication and therapy can be made more effective, for both the users and dispensers of help.

Chapter Three

Breaking Barriers to Intimacy

In the last two chapters, we described the various ways in which barriers and isolating mechanisms are learned, usually as children, to defend against an emotionally destructive environment. The adult, having left that environment, still uses those barriers and mechanisms in his dealings with other people even though they are no longer appropriate. The result is loneliness, anger, and depression. To break through these barriers is difficult. Some people spend years in therapy and end up with their barriers intact. Others seek medication, which treats the symptoms but does not change the behavior.

Most often, people with the kinds of problems indicated above do not seek help until some crisis, divorce or job termination, forces them to seek help to deal with the accompanying pain. Like the alcoholic who will not quit until he bottoms out, many people hang on to their childhood behavior patterns with similar tenacity. The opportunity for change comes with the crisis because the pain is so great, it cannot be borne without help. The alcoholic is forced to admit that he is powerless to stop drinking by him. The depressed victim of a broken marriage can, with help, take responsibility for his or her part in the dissolution of the marriage. That opens the individual to the prospect of change to avoid repeating the mistakes of the past.

The usual opening edge in the entrance to intimate relationships is the expression of the sadness that the individual feels as a result not only of the immediate crisis, but a whole lifetime of loneliness. It is extremely beneficial if this is done in a group setting so that the individual can feel, perhaps for the first time in his or her life, the genuine responses of understanding and empathy that usually accompany an authentic expression of pain. That is the secret of the AA success rate; each member makes a public admission of their powerlessness to control their drinking before a group of people who have already admitted to the same problem and readily voice their understanding and acceptance. It is a powerful experience for someone who has spent years in an isolated alcoholic haze to suddenly find a whole group of people who understand and accept him in spite of his drinking.

So too, for the depressed person, to meet a whole group of people who understand his or her sadness is an exhilarating experience. The trick now becomes to go on to explore what the individual needs to do to continue to relate to people in ways designed to regain the closeness of this first experience on a regular basis. It is for this process that a good group leader is crucial, and it is here that AA usually fails because of the tendency of the AA meetings to become mechanical. For once the sadness is revealed, the individual must be guided into an exploration of the roots of that sadness. Along the way, those idiosyncratic ways he has developed to keep people at a distance must be confronted and terminated.

The flip side of sadness is usually anger; long-suppressed anger at a critical parent that may only be at the unconscious level. The immediate anger is directed at the targets the individual blames for his or her misery—the ex-spouse, boss or the whole society. This anger also needs to be expressed in a safe way, and there is no safer place than before a group with a trained leader. The group learns from each other about both expressing anger safely and responding to it. Other feelings should follow once the anger is dispersed. Feeling and expressing these feelings is the second stage in breaking the barriers to effective communication and a movement towards intimacy.

There is nothing magical about the expression of anger and sadness. Most people know that it helps to have someone you can talk to even if there is no therapy beyond that expression. But for people with emotions locked away inside themselves so deeply that they are not fully aware of them and even less likely to admit they are there, getting that anger and sadness out in front of a group is a difficult but vastly rewarding undertaking. It is also important for those listening that their responses be authentic; that is that they clearly express the emotional response that was triggered by what was revealed. To the degree that this kind of communication is fostered, trust is built and the first stages of a capacity for intimacy are built.

This does not mean that the person is transformed—he still

has to work the steps if he is an alcoholic and all the depressed types discussed above have to go through the emotional equivalent of working the steps to make the kinds of changes that will allow them to establish healthy, intimate relations with the people that are important to them (always assuming that those people are capable of responding). But the first and most difficult step has been taken. The first experience with the potential for intimacy with a number of people has been established. The horror of personal revelation has been faced and conquered. What happens next is conditional upon a number of variables, which include:

1. The skill of the group leader in directing towards change.
2. The motivation of the individual; how deeply and how much change is desired.
3. The time available to both group and individual to work on change.

Even given the most opportune of circumstances, the breaking down of a lifetime's worth of barriers to intimacy is a slow but rewarding process. It can give the alcoholic an experience with something else in life other than barroom chatter and the replacement of one addiction with another. The workaholic may pause long enough to find something more rewarding than work to fill his needs and bolster his self-esteem. The perfectionist may find a whole new world where perfection is impossible and all humans are potentially equal. In this world he may at last find the peace and enjoyment that have eluded him in his unyielding attempt to attain perfection at work and at home. For the critics, they will find that it does no good to criticize an emotion—it just is, neither bad nor good. Likewise, it is difficult to advise an emotion; it is there and you either identify with it or you don't. Those who are emotionally detached will begin to understand the benefits of authentic movements towards intimacy; they will learn to put out emotional energy rather than to wait passively for others to approach them.

All these understandings provide entry into to the world of others. The final chapters, four through six, offer insight into the positive side of the intimate experience, moving towards intimacy, intimacy as a cure for depression, and the joys of living intimately.

Chapter Four

Moving Towards Intimacy

As we have seen in Chapter Three, the biggest barriers to intimacy are related to the unexpressed feelings that are hidden or disguised through mechanisms learned usually as children to protect the child's fragile ego from hurt. The result is residue of anger at the parents, sadness about what was wanted and not received, and a degree of depression that periodically emerges when crisis or stress prevents the individual from keeping these feelings repressed. The expression of these feelings of sadness and anger is the first step towards curing the depression and breaking the barriers that separate the individual both from his own feelings and those of others. Beyond that are the whole range of feelings that may be repressed that would add a significant dimension to his life if these too could be brought to the surface; feelings of tenderness, joy, well-being. Confidence, security, togetherness, etc. To begin to feel these things and to express them is one way out of a depressive life style. Even if he does not attain a capacity for intimacy that will allow him to actually achieve an intimate relationship, there is some evidence that suggests that the mere desire to be intimate translates into positive results.

Once the barriers begin to fall, the individual becomes capable of authentic expression. He may have been honest before, but since he was not aware of his feelings, he was not authentic. What he said might have been factually accurate, but no one could tell how he felt. Now his words begin to have a new congruence as the expression of feeling begins to accompany his words. His behavior also is congruent with his words and feelings. He then becomes emotionally available. Understanding his own emotions, he begins to feel with others; to relate their emotions to his own. He becomes emotionally responsive. He can give and receive emotional support. He has passed through the three basic components of intimate communication; assessing his feelings, articulating them, and putting out the energy towards others that is reflective of what he is feeling. He is ready for an intimate relationship with a significant other, providing, of course that his partner is emotionally available as well.

Assuming that both partners have learned the skills necessary for an intimate relationship—that they both are authentic in their dealings with each other—most problems can be worked out in equitable manner so that neither feels dominated. In fact, problems can be seen as opportunities for intimacy as each can tell the other how they feel about an issue and expect the depth of that feeling to be understood and respected. It is not so important what the problem is but how the partner feels about it that is important. Hence the ability to express and respond to feelings is the key to intimate communication. This is especially important in their sexual relationship.

Feelings about sex run deep and practically everyone has been subjected to some sexual repression. The goal is to make sex mutually satisfying. To reach it, each has to know the other both physically and emotionally. Most couples are bound to find some differences in attitude, needs, orgasmic abilities, and responsiveness. To work these out so that both are satisfied takes a lot of discussion, mutual respect, and authentic expression.

Women used to viewing sex as a weapon to gain the things that they want from men will have difficulty adjusting to an authentic exchange on sexual needs. Men, who view sex simply from their need to achieve an orgasm, may find the idea of making sex pleasurable for his partner strange. Both may have difficulty defining what it is they want out of their sexual exchanges.

To make these kinds of revelations and then work out adjustments requires skill and sensitivity. Problems such as where to place the television set diminish to insignificance in the face of the challenges of mutual sexual satisfaction. And, once the latter is achieved other problems are not as likely to be quite so disturbing. No other area provides the couple with the opportunity to so completely melt the boundaries between them. With the intimate sex act, a joining of the physical, emotional and spiritual components of the relationship can take place. It can be the most beautiful expression of their love that is available to humans.

Still, even though their boundaries melt in the sexual act as in no other experience, the fact they recognize their individual differences and preferences and respect them helps maintain their respective identities and their individual integrity. Neither is exploited nor manipulated. No loss of dignity or self-esteem takes place. Boundaries are not so much lowered as temporarily merged. It makes the sex act a mutual celebration of their relationship. It then offers a central restorative and invigorating medium for the rejoining of the couple after separation, either physically or because of disagreement.

Likewise, in other areas where the couple merges, in the arranging of the house, yard, the birthing and raising of children, authentic expressions of feelings with mutual respect and empathetic responses will both give the couple an identity while respecting individual differences. Such respect carries over into their mutual careers, individual families, and past experiences—information about all these is shared with the other but the experience is part of what gives each partner a separate identity and the boundaries here are legitimate. Hence, the intimate couple has no secrets from each other, but they do maintain their separate identities, which are respected by the other. But to build such a relationship, one must first find and attract someone who is emotionally available and has the skills necessary to build an intimate relationship. How do you tell? Unfortunately, there is no substitute for communication designed to find out how he will respond. Will he talk about his feelings as well as respond to yours? Is it authentic or is it just the expression without the actual feeling behind the words? Is his body language congruent with his words? Does he show respect for your individual tastes, your history, your family, and your career? Is he interested in how you feel about all manner of things or does he just state his feelings? Or, the reverse of that, does he just ask about your feelings and not reveal his own?

Probably most important is the ability to put forth the energy to pursue the emotional response he desires in an authentic way. Does he do this with consistency or does he wait for you to provide the emotional energy? Because of their conditioning, men are generally slower to respond emotionally than women. Hence, a certain amount of patience is required if women want to relate emotionally to their mate. Above all, they must avoid imposing their emotions on their mate. Just as the male if he is more rational will have to be patient and not relate to his wife as an emotional child incapable of rational thought the woman must avoid treating her husband as a computer incapable of demonstrating emotion. If they are on different levels in their capacities to express emotions, they must work to learn from each other and grow mutually.

Another key to good relationships lies in the ability to express dissatisfactions, irritations and disagreements before they develop into real problems and produce angry withdrawal. During the romantic period, not much is expressed except statements of love and approval. Inevitably, however, as each partner becomes more aware of the other, the negative features of each personality become obvious to the other. The expression of these unpleasant facts of life is difficult at best and impossible for those who live in fear that their lover will leave them. In any case it has to be handled delicately so that the mate will not feel blamed or criticized.

One key to initiating the process is to squarely face the fact that the problem is yours. You are the one that cannot stand the mess in the bathroom that your mate does not see. The mess may represent an early fear that the love of a parent may be lost because of it. An indication that your mate is not going to protect you from messes and the loss of love that you may fear might result.

What is wanted is the aid of your mate in resolving your problem. Most people in love are eager to please and will do whatever is necessary to maintain the relationship as long as the request is made in terms that is neither criticizing nor blaming and the invitation to respond to requests from the other is a clear part of what is expressed. You usually will not threaten someone by merely making clear what you are feeling and inviting them to share their own problems so that something can be worked out that will allow both to emerge as winners.

In this case, merely expressing the fear of messes as they relate to childhood threats of the loss of parental love might place the problem in perspective so that both can face the problem with understanding, criticism can be avoided, the threat of losing love can be reduced, and the mess seen as an easily remedied problem rather than the basis for a divorce.

Such an approach, should keep the relationship on solid ground where basic love is affirmed, responsibility for one's own feelings is assessed, and plans are made to smooth over those areas where feelings diverge. If you feel positive about all of the above questions as applied to both yourself and your prospective mate, then the chances are pretty good you can establish an intimate relationship. What follows is a list of hints about what some people do to confuse the issue.

1. Some people confuse honesty with authenticity. A "head" person may be honestly dealing with facts while keeping his feelings hidden. Watch for both the words and the emotions and see if they are congruent.

2. Some people are strictly goal oriented. A goal-directed person may appear interested in you for his own purposes—he wants a well-groomed wife to aid with his career goals—to help raise his children—to share the cost of living, etc. Watch for the degree to which your goals are respected and you are valued in a way that recognizes your complete identity and the authenticity of that recognition.

3. Some people smile inappropriately even while expressing sadness. This is an indication that something is wrong. Watch for the congruency of body language with verbal expression.

4. Some people lecture rather than relate. This may be an indication that they are going to try to control you. Look for someone who will share their thoughts and feelings and respects yours even about trivial things.

5. Some don't know what they want. They will try to make you do all the decision making so that they can coast and criticize. Look for someone who will share their opinions and their feelings about what they want.

6. Some people have difficulty admitting their behavior is anything less than perfect and will refuse to assess their role in the development of any problem and place the blame squarely on you, especially if you admit to having a problem. Look for someone who will admit to being human with all the potential for error that the human condition fosters.

7. Some people know what they want but only in an unconscious unexpressed way. Watch out for non-verbal expressions of power such as withdrawal and silence about wants and needs.

There are, as everyone knows, no guarantees in life. But, hopefully, by following the hints given above you may find someone who is capable of the kind of intimate relationship most of us want;

or, at least, is willing to try.

Chapter Five

Intimacy as a cure for Depression

In Chapter 2, we looked at depression in terms of isolation and looked at various ways in which people isolate themselves—drugs, work, body language, seeking perfection, being critical, or preaching. We saw that these methods usually are learned in childhood as a survival technique. They are inappropriate to adult life, and, though they will work in the short term, eventually some crisis, divorce or dismissal, will necessitate self-examination and depression can result.

The signs of depression are easy to spot. They are:

1. Sadness
2. Decreased interest in life
3. Weight fluctuation
4. Sleep disturbance
5. Feelings of worthlessness and hopelessness
6. Fatigue
7. Concentration problems
8. Death fears or suicidal thoughts

The way out of depression is in a movement towards getting more of the things that make life pleasurable. Of these, more intimate relations are most important to mental health. To get there, in chapter 3, we indicated that first steps involved breaking through the barriers to self-expression, that sadness expressed authentically before a group that responds with empathy and has a leader trained to enhance the opportunities for such expression and to carry that breakthrough into other areas. The individual sees that he is not alone with his problem—others have similar ones or even worse. He has been authentic perhaps for the first time since early childhood and unlike that experience his disclosure of his feelings has had a positive effect. For the first time as an adult, he has shared intimate feelings with other people. His barrier has been broken, but he is still far from being emotionally available.

He has made a movement that could lead to the establishment of intimate relationships, but he has only been intimate once and then under extreme circumstances. He could panic and leave. He could use his new skill to gain sympathy, to "talk depression" at every available opportunity; thus, prolonging his own depression, and avoiding the undertaking of those personal changes that would help keep him from repeating the problem. That is where the skill of the leader can be crucial. The leader must guide the still-depressed group member back to the roots of the problem and show him ways of overcoming them. He is likely to have a number of barriers to intimacy that have accumulated over the years. He will have to get in touch with other feelings besides sadness and learn how to express them authentically. He must experience intimacy and practice it in a safe environment before he is ready to use these skills in the world. His guilt feelings must be diminished though a realistic assessment of responsibility much like the AA's Step Four in which a personal inventory is taken of personal strengths and weaknesses and past debts recognized. All of this is done before the group so that he is validated as a person by the responses of the group. This process is designed to raise his self-esteem as he develops a more realistic sense of his own identity, and, along with that, a more realistic look at his own needs. His past activities, which were designed to avoid feeling, must be moderated to allow him to make judgments based on what feels good and what doesn't feel good. He must learn to express these feelings, to take his stand, to risk being himself. The more he does this, the higher his self-esteem will rise and along with it his confidence in being able to defend his own interests. When that comes he can discard those childish mechanisms of withdrawing, blaming, criticizing, escaping, demanding or somehow controlling that caused him so much grief in the past.

He now knows that intimacy feels good, that depression feels bad, and, that he cannot have intimacy and continues his perfectionist, workaholic, alcoholic, critical, judgmental behavior. He also knows that such behavior led him to a crisis, which triggered his depression. He cannot have intimacy if he either controls or is controlled by his mate. He has learned that the process of moving towards intimacy; revealing his feelings, defining his preferences, and making a stand on who he is, can help him avoid the destructive behavior of the past, and, hence the isolation that led to his depression. To get to a point where he has a clear understanding of his behavior, he must have explored its roots in the family system he grew up with. He must see how the style of life maintained by his parents affect his own expectations. Chances are that he seeks the familiar in his mate selection. The mate need not be a duplicate of his mother. But it is almost certain that he will not be comfortable with those behavior patterns, which are not familiar. He must be clear about how those things that are different about his mate are creating a problem for him. There also are probably things about his mate that are negative that remind him of his parents. These things, especially the mate who marries a critical person like his critical parent, will cause special problems. Rubbing a raw spot in a mate that is there because of years of being worked over by a parent is sure to generate a lot of negative feelings. Unless both mates are aware of where these trouble spots are, they are not likely to understand the emotion-charged responses of their mate when difficulty in these areas emerges.

Intimate living requires, perhaps more than anything else, a level of awareness and an ability to empathize that is inherent in most humans. Unfortunately, many family systems crush the natural human capacity to live intimately by creating repressive environments where the child cannot remain whole. To live healthily, trust, spontaneity, and unconditional love have to be brought back into the family. Then the individual can work on reawakening those parts of himself that he has repressed and begin to live intimately without depression.

Chapter Six

Living Intimately

For many people, especially those types described in Chapter 2, the concept of intimacy has either been not understood at all or considered unattainable. The expression of feelings was never thought a safe thing to do. Isolation from others had become a way of life. What relations were established were contractual and based on the necessities of living. These people either controlled others or were controlled by them. The prospect of an equal relationship based on mutual respect for the identity of the other and the authentic sharing of feelings and information about themselves was not part of their understanding of the possibilities of human existence. Many lived long and outwardly productive lives without ever experiencing an intimate relationship. But for others, something triggered depression and the years of isolation and disguised sadness came to fruition in the characteristics of depression described in Chapter 5. Like the alcoholic, the individual "bottoms out" and admits his depression is out of his control and seeks help. At that point there are many alternatives. He can be given a pill and sent away. He can get pills and individual or group therapy or all three. He may choose to tough it out by himself without fully realizing what is happening to him. He may turn to books and articles like this one to try to help himself.

Learning to be intimate in some ways is like learning to swim; you have to get into the water to learn how to do it. Reading about swimming or intimacy will not get you there. Our hope, however, is that you may discover where the pools are and what tactics and procedures are involved. Knowing this can save you time and help you over your fear of the water. What follows is a description of the possibilities inherent in living intimately.

Intimacy, as we have seen requires certain skills. One must be able to talk authentically and to listen responsively. The intimate couple knows how each feels and if they do not they simply have to ask. There is a faith and trust that has to be built that each is speaking and responding authentically—that there is congruence between what they are saying and how they feel. There are areas of feeling and doing where the commonality of the couple merges into togetherness so that their boundaries as individuals are temporarily blurred and the two become as one. These areas grow with the relationship until that relationship has a life of its own.

This process is of course not free of conflict. Different values, life styles and preferences have to be worked out. They must be expressed with feeling appropriate to the degree of importance the matter has to both. Responsibility must be assessed and the conflict resolved through compromise or acceptance. Tolerance for differences is inherent in the intimate relationship. Problems are seen as exercises in intimacy that offers opportunity to grow and stretch the relationship beyond its current boundaries.

There are numerous exercises that are designed to promote intimacy. Perhaps the simplest is the exchanging of lists by couples of positive specific ways their mate can please them containing such things as activities each likes to do with the other, places to go, things to eat, etc. Then each couple gives something to the other that is on the list every day. The obvious result is that each gets to know the other better and receives an almost sure-fired avenue towards making the other feel positive towards you. Each gets nurtured in a way they have stated that they like. A positive nurturing environment is created to replace the old power struggle.

The exercise can then get more complicated as the couple progresses into sensitive sexual areas and exchanges of fantasies. The basic principle being that each gets to know the other better to expand the areas of mutually shared pleasure and an understanding of sensitive issues to be explored. As the relationship goes and the couple becomes more intimate, requests for behavioral changes can be made. The exchange of family memories is one tool that will make the areas of potential sensitivity clearer. Recollections of a cold, unresponsive mother can go a long way towards explaining the profound needs for affection exhibited by a mate. Similarly, the child who grows up under the too-watchful eye of a mother who will not trust her out of her sight will help explain the sensitivity of women or men who emerge from that environment to the restraints, real or imagined, she or he finds in a new relationship.

"Mirroring" is a commonly used assignment for promoting communication. One partner simply reflects the thoughts and feelings expressed by the other, as he understands them in turn. The benefits are obvious; misunderstandings are corrected immediately, feelings and thoughts can be shared, and each feels listened to and understood. Communication is promoted as a two way street and a feeling of equality is established.

All such exercises expand the areas of shared experience and extend the boundaries of the relationship. At the same time the boundaries of the relationship are changing, individual boundaries also are growing as self-awareness grows. Each partner must be flexible enough to allow for changes as the relationship grows and each member of the couple undergoes changes. Implicit in this is the self-evident maxim that each must stay in touch with other so that changes are voiced and worked out to the satisfaction of both. Differences are recognized and respected as part of the others identity.

Neither should try to control the other either overtly or passively. Decisions should be made through a loving use of the accepted methods for negotiation. The tools of decision-making are authentic appraisal, negotiation, compromise, tolerance and acceptance. Differences are aired and responses are expressed and hopefully the road to settlement makes the relationship stronger as differences become more deeply known and respected. As the world exists now, it is not possible to extend these rules to everyone that is a working associate or social acquaintance. There are situations on the job where orders must be given or obeyed without question or the job will be lost. Similarly some social acquaintances cannot handle intimacy. Hence, barroom chatter must suffice for some social occasions. But for those special friends and fellow workers who can be trusted, intimate relations can provide a way to make both work and play more satisfying.

Skill at recognizing authenticity in others will help you make friends and discover those who would con you with a facade of superficial feeling that does not penetrate to any deeper level than surface expression. The ultimate goal of many of the world's great political philosophers has been to create a logical structure that would promote the kinds of communities that would provide the maximum opportunity for loving relationships based on some social organization that would end the striving for control, which has been a dominant feature of human history. Freud also looked at the problem in his "Eros and Civilization" and gave up in despair of ever resolving the basic irrationality he saw at the root of human social behavior. Wilhelm Reich, one of Freud's imminent disciples made an attempt to combine Freudian principles with the rational utopianism of Karl Marx. However, his initial works were lost in the west in its descent into a neurotic anticommunism and in the Communist bloc because of its dismissal of Freudian psychology. It may be time for the world to revive that effort.

Until then, we make no utopian claims for the intimate relationship and its capacity to make the world a better place. It is likely, however, that establishing intimate relationships may make your individual world better for you and those you relate to. The existence of a world free from depression is a goal that, for now, must be addressed one person at a time.

In the next chapter I describe how I worked my own way out of a rebellious and depressed life style.

Chapter Seven

Depression and Rebellion

According to Ernest Gruen, the distinguished author of a perceptive little book entitled, *The Search For Self*, a person must rebel or never experience a self of their own. Earlier the French existentialist writer, Albert Camus, had said it more succinctly, "I exist, therefore, I rebel." Without rebellion, we are doomed to belong to those who structured our psychic being, our family, our church, the business we work for, or even the country we pledge our allegiance to. To develop our own identity, separation from those imposed value structures and the conditioned behaviors that went with them is necessary.

But the kind of rebellion that occurs is all important. Some rebellion that is based merely on anger can be counterproductive and the person involved may merely swap one set of poisonous leaders for another. According to Gruen, the attitude of the rebelling person is all-important; the rebellion must be based on love and sympathy. If not, a real identity may not develop, as the individual looks not within himself but outward to find groups of similarly angry people to give his life direction. Street gangs depend on this form of rebellion as a source of membership, so do radical religious groups, political parties, and sectarian groups of all types.

Rebellion based on love and sympathy allows the individual to pick and choose those elements in his environment he wants to discard as toxic to his personal growth and those, which he wishes to retain as part of his own worldview. He can retain those parts of the family value system that he feels serves him and discard those that do not. He can enter and leave the family without joining the system and responding in the old ways. He is his own master. But, until his separation process is emotionally complete, he may travel great distances without truly leaving home.

There is a profound difference between rebellion in the classic angry sense and the separation from the system based on love and empathy that is essential for the development of autonomous individuals. My own experience, until recently, was restricted to the angry rebellion category. I went through most of the classic phases, being disruptive in school, joining gangs outside of school, smoking, drinking, gambling and generally being both self-destructive and non-contributory. I straightened out sufficiently while in the military to make use of the G.I. Bill and get into college. There I wandered aimlessly from one major to another until I discovered historical rebellion and the opportunity to participate first hand through protests against war in general and then against Vietnam in particular. This led to participation in the Civil Rights movement and a general understanding of the plight of the poor and oppressed in American life and an identification with whatever movement popped up to do something in their name. This provided a ready focus for my anger and a reason for continuing my academic career. Academics were needed to recruit cadre for the movement and to provide studies which would further the understanding of the revolutionary process. That kept me busy enough to avoid dealing with my underlying problems with depression and a lack of self-esteem. It also allowed me to neglect my woefully inadequate social abilities and provided a ready excuse for failed relationships. The revolution was important, I was not. Relationships and family were not important either.

Until recently, I had no idea there were psychological reasons for this behavior stemming from the lack of affection, love, and support in my family system. Rather than confronting that system, something that is not safe for a child to do, I first tried to please my parents with academic prowess. This never worked so I withdrew from the system and rebelled. Reading about revolutionaries, who had gone before me, such as, the famed Russian revolutionary, Lenin, provided me with inspiration and direction. Like me, Lenin seemed to be a classic example of the results of rebellion based on anger. Lenin's anger was directed outward by the example of his brother who had thrown himself into the ant-Tsarist movement of the late nineteenth century. His brother was finally hanged as part of a failed attempt to assassinate the Tsar. Lenin, hence forward, dedicated himself to transforming the Russian government through revolution.

One of Lenin's key ideas was based on the experiences of

himself and his brother; the organizational principle that, in Russia, only professional revolutionaries could survive. Therefore, he advocated the development of a small, but highly trained group of revolutionaries who would devote their entire beings to the task of overthrowing the government. All personal decisions, about where to live, who to pick for a mate, even down to what to read and what music to listen had to be based on furthering his revolutionary goals. Aspects of his life that interfered with his single-minded devotion were cast aside. Lenin gave up listening to classic music like Beethoven's sonatas, because he claimed, the music made you feel good and you would stroke your dog. This according to Lenin might eventually get your hand bitten. He even gave up his beloved chess games because they took time away from his revolutionary work.

Lenin gathered men around him who shared these views and molded together the Bolshevik Party. The guiding leadership principles he developed for the Bolsheviks, were based on what came to be known as democratic centralism. Ideas were discussed freely at lower levels and suggestions about the direction the party should take were sent upward to a central committee chaired by Lenin. Once the central committee decided an issue, the party position was established and no deviation was permitted. For those who wanted both a sense of belonging and firm leadership the situation was ideal, but individual identity became blurred and autonomy was not permitted.

We do not know enough about Lenin's family to say with certainty where the roots of his own rebellion and that of his brother came from. Lenin's father was a minor bureaucrat and there is no record of his indulging in any criticism of the government he worked for. He does not seem to have been an especially cruel or authoritarian father. Never the less, something in the family caused both Lenin and his brother to turn against the state in a militant and dramatic way. Neither followed in the footsteps of their father. Perhaps the answer lies with their mother who exerted pressure for her sons to do better than their relatively weak father. Lacking both affection from the mother and without a strong father figure to identify with, both brothers turned their immense talents against the state, which afforded a readily available target for their anger at not getting what they needed from their family.

At any rate, it is certain that the revolution that Lenin led was not inspired by love and sympathy. Once in power, Lenin held on steadfastly, even bending Marxist ideology to fit that need to retain power. Compromises were made with the autocratic Germans so that the war could be halted. Democracy was ended and the elected representatives of the people sent home. Civil war at home and invasion from abroad caused extreme measures to be taken in the interest of survival. The army and secret police grew in strength and importance. Such actions allowed men like Stalin to rise in the party hierarchy as the ability to carry out ruthless actions came to be valued at the expense of the humanist elements of Marxist philosophy.

To Lenin's credit it must be said that towards the end of his life he seemed to realize what he had created and made some effort to prevent the rise of Stalin. He took steps to compromise the militant war communism he had supported while the new Soviet state was under attack. But he was already a sick man and his efforts were too little and too late. In effect, the ultimate result was the triumph of Stalin and the replacement of one set of authoritarian bureaucrats with another.

My own infatuation with Lenin and the concept of total devotion to the cause of revolution blinded me to the obvious problems with supporting such a system. Stalin was discussed endlessly in the college circles I frequented, but mainly his excesses were excused as necessary given the times. "If only Lenin had lived," was the most frequently heard lament on the left. But the Stalin problem is a key to understanding a basic flaw that plagues those groups that attract individuals where angry rebellion is a key motivation for joining the group.

Unlike Lenin and most of the early Marxists who were imbued with a western ethical humanism, Stalin's rebellion, as Alice Miller has pointed out, was not tempered with humanist ideology or individual compassion. Stalin was exposed only to unrelenting brutality in his own family. He knew only the use and abuse of power. His family background was excellent training for the rough and tumble of war and revolution. No kindly Aunts and Uncles were available to Stalin to moderate the abuse he received from his own family and would later dish out to his own people. Even his own family was not immune from his violence and his wife eventually committed suicide. Once in power, Stalin, returned to the system of values inherited from his family and ruled without pity as he had been ruled in his family system. He was in a word, a brute, but he was smart enough to cover his brutality with a smattering of revolutionary ideology.

So did Hitler. Miller draws a similar portrait of Hitler who was abused by his father. He then seeks power primarily to emulate his abusive father. Both Stalin and Hitler played up their leader roles as far as possible and both drew heavily from that part of the population which had been trained to obey authoritarian father figures and were quite willing to lose themselves in the state bureaucracy where only unquestioned loyalty was demanded. Miller uses Adolph Eichmann, the man who ran Dachau, as an example of the super compliant bureaucrat par excellence, who, after being captured by the Israelis, was so afraid of the results of independent action that he even asked permission to move his bowels after being seated on the toilet. Angry rebellion or complete denial of self is two possible responses to the authoritarian system.

The psychological problem that develops is that the individual who rebels out of anger is still responding to the system and he really has not separated himself from it. Stalin and Hitler represent two extreme responses to brutality experienced in the family system. They both rebel, but when given an opportunity to structure a system of their own, they revert to brutality similar and even worse than what they experienced in their family systems. This capacity for brutal behavior affects both the deranged rebel leader—Hitler and Stalin—and the obsequious non-rebelling followers they surround themselves with. The brute factor plagued the rebellions of the sixties, especially as the sixties started to wane and the war continued abroad and the civil rights movement bogged down in economic problems that seem irresolvable.

In the beginning, most of the leaders of the protest movement came out of highly ethical environments, church people like Martin Luther King and the Christian Leadership Conference, A.J. Muste and the War Resister's League, and the Committee for Non-Violent Action. As the sixties progressed, angrier, more violent groups appeared and dominated both movements. The Black Panthers and the Weathermen typified the new rebellion of anger. In the tense environment of the late sixties, the brute factor began to weigh heavily on what had been a highly ethical cause conducted for the most part within the boundaries of humanist or Jeffersonian response to readily apparent injustice.

The brutes were encouraged by FBI agent provocateurs under J. Edgar Hoover who were eager to discredit both groups and who had a special hatred for Martin Luther King. The line between legitimate protest and criminal behavior grew blurred. Peaceful demonstrations turned into trashings, windows broken and shops looted. Leadership fell out the hands of the old, religious types and a younger, angrier group took over.

My own participation in the anti-war movement at the University of Wisconsin became confused. Ideologically I supported the younger angrier groups, but temperamentally I was not suited to rock throwing or trashing. Pulled in both directions, I tried to do both, the intellectual work required by the old school and the demonstrating required by the new. Attracted by violence and seeing it as a necessary response to the violence being afflicted on the victims of the system and the increasing use of police and the National Guard to restrain demonstrators, I was scared and repelled by the brutes on both sides. Fortunately, my studies took me overseas and away from the dilemma. The Black Power movement had already expelled white participants like me. By the end of the sixties we were pretty much limited to cheerleaders and fundraisers for the Panthers. By the time I returned to the states in 1969, the violence of the 1968 Chicago Convention and the bombing of the Physics Lab at the University of Wisconsin signaled the retreat of the left and the end of most of the anti-war activity around Madison. The brutes on both sides had finally caused the nation to turn away from war both at home and abroad. Any remaining appetite was put to rest by the antics of the weathermen in Chicago and the National Guard at Kent State. I was safe to retreat to the books. But my rebelliousness was still there; ready to boil to the surface whenever a "cause" provoked me. Finding little to do in Wisconsin, I left for small Black college in Arkansas to recruit cadre and to wait the next phase of the revolution. Scott Peck has described the dynamics of a process on the war scene in Vietnam similar to what was happening at home. In an appendix to his book, "People of the Lie", he explains the brutality of the Mai Lai massacre. The massacre occurred because the troops involved were primarily career soldiers, trained to obey without question. When ordered to shoot women and children by James Calley, their neurotic first lieutenant, they obeyed. Rebellion might have occurred, Peck claims, if a detachment composed largely of draftees from all walks of life had been involved. These men, or at least those who retained their sense of autonomy, would have rebelled against performing the inhumane act requested of them. That theme is also seen in Oliver Stone's movie, *Platoon*, where it is the college-educated volunteer who objects to the treatment of captured Vietnamese villagers while the regular Army "grunts" passively acquiesce in the brutality committed by the platoon bully. They refuse to challenge the system. The hero not only rebels against the system but also takes action to change it and it nearly costs him his life. This act of rebellion, which requires enormous courage and is the essence of loving and empathetic rebellion, is made easier because the college boy is never fully integrated in to the system—he is part of it but yet remains aloof. To rebel from within the system is extremely difficult. Witness, for example the relatively small number of white southerners who were active participants in the civil rights movement. Many more southerners attempted to distance themselves from the more red neck elements in there midst and remained silent because the costs for those who were active and vocal were quite high. In a way, silent withdrawal is a return to childish ways of dealing with adult repression—a defense mechanism that serves the child well allowing survival given the overwhelming power of adults, but, when used as an adult, passive withdrawal has its costs in loss of self esteem and the inability to respond appropriately to all manner of challenges that are raised by the society one lives in.

According to Thomas Jefferson and many of America's Founding Fathers, sometimes rebellion is the appropriate response. That basic truth lies behind the famous Jeffersonian quotation about the necessity for the "tree of Liberty to be watered every twenty years with the blood of rebels." Unfortunately for the tree of liberty, not many rebels willing to shed their blood have stepped forward. Passive separation from conflict with authorities was, for Jefferson, a coward's way out. The contemporary system raises many rebels, but relatively few who rebel out of love and empathy and even fewer who are willing to shed their blood for the cause of liberty. The angry rebellion of street gangs has become quite common, but that rebellion is nihilistic and provides merely a training ground for brutes and their leaders. To Jefferson, rebellion was an intellectual reaction against the existence of oppression to be followed by positive action. The Declaration of Independence is mostly a list of those perceived evils which violated the natural rights that Jefferson claimed were inherent in the human condition. The right to this kind of rebellion was placed in most of the state constitutions of the period. Among the sophisticated gentlemen who became the Founding Fathers and the British aristocrats who they fought, there never was any disagreement about ends and means. The war was fought out according to the rules of the era. It had brutal aspects, but, overall, the confrontation was never controlled by brutes. The leaders for the most part were guided by ethical rules of conduct developed over generations. Jefferson's later writings indicate that he was concerned over the ability of future generations to protect their inherent rights as the Federal government solidified its control over the new nation. Like Jefferson, Gruen, Miller, and Peck, each sees the potential for great destruction in the development of individuals without a full sense of self, trained only to obey, without self esteem, and unable to choose between ethical and unethical courses of conduct. They are ready to follow the brutes among them who can convince them that the sources of their problems are outside themselves—in the conspiracies of blacks, Jews, Communists—this gives focus to their anger and explains the roots of their problems.

Earlier studies by Eric Fromm, Victor Frankel and Bruno Bettleheim, all survivors of German concentration camps, have stressed the necessity for self esteem, a sense of meaning, a love for freedom and willingness to make choices to preserve it as vital to the health of individuals and society. Somehow these three men were able to grow up in German society and still develop into autonomous individuals, able to live according to their own ethical systems while the world around the went crazy.

They all, in their way, support rebellion from the authoritarian family and state as necessary for the development of the individual's autonomy and independent identity. Each, also, stresses the necessity for humanist rebellion based on empathy and love. The rebellion then is not one that inspires destruction, but one that allows the development of an autonomous individual through separation from a system that threatens his growth into an autonomous individual, one who recognizes his right to choose and become his own person—he rebels against choices made for him by his parents or the state that do not conform to his system of ethics or that stunt his growth by controlling his behavior. It is that system of ethics that gives his life meaning and it was a highly developed sense of meaning that allowed Victor Frankel to survive the rigors of a Nazi concentration camp while others succumbed to malaise and hopelessness.

Such a person cannot be forced to indulge in behavior that violates that code. Since it is based on the humanist values of love and empathy, he respects the autonomy of others and is unwilling to violate it in any way. Hence he allows others the right to choose that he demand for himself. His sons and daughters are taught, not to obey without question, but to question and choose among alternatives. They learn they are responsible for their choices and for whatever happens as a result of their choices. They are taught not to wish to "escape from Freedom" but to cherish it and embrace the responsibilities it entails. These general principles are applicable to relationships between individuals as well as for confronting systems of authority. It is no accident that Eric Fromm who is the source of many of these ideas is also the author of The Art of Loving.

Mindless neurotic rebellion develops when the individual finds it necessary to rebel but does not have the self-esteem or ethical system that allows him to make choices that enhance his own development. Without the internal compass to steer him, the neurotic rebel may find himself trapped in cycles of revolt and repression that are destructive to both himself and the society he lives in and lead to depression and further decrease his self-esteem. His rebellion is uncontrolled and addictive since he is not making choices at all but responding only to the need to separate himself from the system he feels is oppressing him. To escape that cycle and end the loneliness and depression it brings, he may join any number of groups that offer mindless rebellion from parental values in exchange for unquestioning allegiance—a street gang, a political party, or a religious or political sect. These are the unfortunate individuals who seek out gurus and causes to fill the emptiness in their lives. Ultimately they are disillusioned with their chosen gurus and their organizations because they only offer temporary relief from their loneliness. Sooner or later, he rebels again and turns against the organization only to seek another in its place. None give the genuine human contact he needs, and none fills the desire for genuine love and empathy which can only grow out of intimate contact with other autonomous individuals. He is in a sense not much different from his brothers who throw themselves into mindless (or, perhaps selfless is the more appropriate term) obedience to business or government.

Neurotic rebellion can take a frightful toll both on the individual involved and the society he finds himself in if the rebellion that it generates takes a destructive or violent turn. Street gangs are the obvious example. Political rebellion is more complicated. Both Lenin and Stalin accomplished much by totally devoting their energies to rebellion and then running revolutionary governments. But because each (Stalin to a greater degree than Lenin) was capable of forgetting the human dimension in their rebellion—purging their political beings from complicating questions of human compassion—they each ended by doing a great deal of damage to their countrymen and to the future of their revolution. Each when faced with the responsibilities of governing turned back to the moral structures left to him by his family. In Stalin case this meant virtually no compassion at all since all he had known as a child was brutality. With Lenin the record is more complicated, as we have seen, he was not devoid of compassion and was capable of compromise.

The personal payment for such total devotion to rebellion is high. In personal terms, both Lenin and Stalin paid highly for their success. The self-sacrificing behavior that they developed as rebels followed them into political office and their personal relationships were sacrificed to the cause leaving them alone and, it is safe to assume, often depressed. Lenin died young never really tasting the fruits of his accomplishments. Stalin lived longer but his was from all appearances not a happy life. But Lenin and Stalin are exceptional because they were politically successful. For most rebels, the historical record is replete with those who fail and ultimately meet an early death, as did Lenin's brother. Jail sentences, exile, and various forms of more subtle political persecution, such as the blacklists imposed on suspected Communists and fellow travelers in the 1950's in America. Even when the revolt is successful, the rebel is usually constitutionally unable to adapt and is an embarrassment in the period of stability that follows. The hero of the American Revolution, Tom Paine, was scorned and isolated and ended up leaving America and traveling to England and France during the post revolutionary period. Sam Adams ended up as the town drunk. Successful revolutionary leaders are often wary of those they led into rebellion. They are always afraid of that innate capacity to revolt. Because of this, Stalin purged most of the old guard revolutionaries, as did Robespierre before him in the French Revolution.

For rebels in America in recent times, their fate has been to be isolated and ignored. Except for brief periods in the 1930's and again in the 1960's, the dominating capitalist ethos has withstood all challenges by simply absorbing rebels like a huge blotter. For those who believed that the special opportunities created by the crises of depression in the 1930's and the war in Vietnam in the 1960's would result in qualitative changes in the system of power in the United States, the years that followed were bitter disappointments. Harvey Swados has captured the special pathos that keep the faith long after there was any chance of that faith bearing any results in his book about of America's aging radicals from the 1930's entitled, *Standing Fast*. The book's heroes, a band of ex-Trotskyites, sink into lives fraught with unemployment and futility. A similar fate awaited the rebels from the sixties. Abbie Hoffman is perhaps the most famous example of the sixties' rebel who was not able to bear the reactionary age of Reagan and took his own life. Unbearable depression is part and parcel of life for a rebel who has no place to take his anger except to turn it in on himself and those closest to him.

My own experience paralleled Abbie Hoffman's. Although never a public figure like Abbie, I was sucked into the same vortex of action and rebellion with the expectation that a qualitative difference would result from all the effort poured into changing the system. Instead of a new society, we had to endure long years under Nixon and Reagan with a brief respite under Jimmy Carter who didn't bring any qualitative changes and was not much of an improvement over Nixon. During the whole period I suffered through lost jobs, a bout with alcoholism, three broken marriages, and a recurrent depression that ebbed and flowed along with my relationships. During the entire period I never said goodbye to the concept of revolution and rebellion. I replayed the story of Swados' novel and thought seriously several times of joining Abbie Hoffman in the ultimate rebellion, suicide. Only after extensive analysis did it slowly dawn on me that this futile self-destructive behavior was aimed at my parents—that my anger at them that I had transferred to society impelled me just as surely as the craving for alcohol motivates the alcoholic. Unlike Hoffman, I decided to shake the monkey off my back and to live out the rest of my time with whatever dignity I could muster—trying to retain what I could of the ethical code that impel those who fight for justice while shucking the addictive behavior of the angry rebel. That meant going back for a loving and empathetic examination of my roots and new separation based on that love.

At the same time it was necessary to reevaluate part of the accepted revolutionary code, those parts which had plagued me and the rest of the rebels who tried to maintain their commitment in non-revolutionary periods. For example, it became increasingly apparent that the standard concept of revolutionary morality best expressed by Trotsky in his famous debate with educator John Dewey as, "that which aids the revolution is moral," is a pretty useless guide in a non revolutionary period unless you are a criminal—then it provides a ready rationalization for all manner of acts against society—the kind of thinking that prevailed among the Weathermen and the captors of Patty Hearst, the Symbionese Liberation Front. As a substitute for this concept, I was attracted to John Dewey's famous rejoinder, "that which aids the individual to become more humane is moral." I had learned that Trotsky's dictum that all is allowed which aids the revolution, allowed the unscrupulous to rise to positions of authority within the rebelling organization and reproduced an authoritarian rule as bad as the old family and government systems it was designed to overthrow. It is to Trotsky's credit that he was one of the first to see this happening and point to the damage being done by Stalin's use of the party bureaucracy in the Soviet Union.

I also saw that the old revolutionary morality ignores the I-Thou relationship of Martin Buber and treats people as objects (I-It relationships) one uses for revolutionary goals. Both Dewey and Trotsky were engaged in revolution and both failed in the immediate sense, but their methodologies were poles apart. Dewey's recognition of the importance of developing autonomy in children by allowing free choice has been buttressed by a large number of important studies by historians and psychologists who have looked into the problems that result from authoritarian practices by families and educational systems.

For example, a recent study by Patrick Ware of Emory University expressed one of the key concepts with a clarity unusual for the usually cliché ridden educational journals. According to Professor Ware, "Children have to learn to say goodbye before they can say hello." Unfortunately this clarity is not sustained for very long as Dr. Ware then lapses into a prolonged discussion of "attachment theory" using complicated psycho-gibberish to repeat what he had put so well in that one sentence. The essential point, however is to buttress Dewey and Rousseau by stressing the importance of developing the child's self esteem in an environment where he is allowed to make choices, hence, freeing the child from the family system where choices were made for him. The other point is that conceivably such separation from the family can be done without the angry rebellion that authoritarian systems breed. The child retains his love and empathy for his family while he develops his own identity and prepares himself for life as an autonomous individual.

Unfortunately, no contemporary educational system, capitalist or communist has really adopted the methodologies necessary to allow children to grow into autonomous and loving individuals. Both systems have fed off the neurotic denial of self that creates individuals ready to sacrifice their humanity for the good of the system.

Any system that denies humanity and the individual in favor of some abstract concept or materialist goal through authoritarian means eventually produces unhappy and alienated individuals, incomplete persons best exemplified by Alice *Millers' Prisoners of Childhood*, Herbert Marcuse's *One Dimensional Man*, and Eric Hoffer's *True Believers*. It matters little whether they are striving towards accumulating wealth and power or revolution, if they are sacrificing their autonomy—their right to choose between alternative actions—or the right to create and maintain the I—Thou relationship in their dealings with the people around them for the goals of a system that is alien to needs of the individuals in it, the end result is similar, loneliness, alienation, and depression. The understanding is not new. It was implicit in the question asked by Jean Jacque Rousseau in the eighteenth century,

"Why is man born free, yet everywhere is in chains?" Rousseau of course was not familiar with the shackles borne by the businessman in his "gray flannel suit" or the Stalinist bureaucrat in his ill-fitting product of the Communist state, but he quite accurately pointed to the use of some citizens as economic objects whose sole preoccupation was to produce wealth to be accumulated by an aristocracy as fundamental to the necessity for chains. Rousseau went on to develop a system of education which would create "natural men" uncorrupted by greed who would lead the world into a new and better age, a theme taken up by John Dewey in his stress on the importance of free and "natural" choice in the progressive classroom.

The late twentieth century use of this insight is to attempt to develop self-esteem in the traditional classroom. The authoritative structure is kept but the destructive effects are moderated, or so it is presumed, by exercises within the system that will bolster the child's sense of self. You can imagine what Rousseau and Dewey would make of such attempts to ice this essentially authoritarian cake. The product of such systems of authority is angry rebellion, withdrawal, and depression. This in turn feeds the need for more massive doses of authority. Hence, we see in the news the creation of school principal heroes who parade in the halls with baseball bats and with increasing emphasis on performance evaluations of both students and teachers who are molded into conformity as dictated by the needs of the economic system. The development of free and happy, autonomous individuals is given lip service in teacher-training courses but usually neglected in practice. Both student and teacher learn that conformity is valued much more than creativity.

The reason for this neglect of the individual is obvious. The creation of autonomy, as we have seen, involves separation from whatever system of control is in operation. Healthy individuals recognize such systems and refuse to be controlled by them. They may join them temporarily as one revisits one's family, but always with the reservation that one is no longer subject to control and is merely there to exchange news, feelings and to relate on an I-Thou basis. But for those still in the system the autonomous individual is threatening—he is beyond control, no longer an obedient citizen—he has escaped into freedom.

True I-Thou relationships are possible only between

autonomous individuals, for those still enmeshed in an old system are still responding not as a complete individual but as a controlled member of that system. None-the-less the autonomous person still relates as though the other person were autonomous since that is what he wishes to encourage and he is independent enough to not allow his actions to be response dependent. To be dependent on the responses of those tied to the system would make the individual responsive to the system itself. In the post-WWII period, a number of studies of totalitarianism appeared, the most famous was Hannah Arendt's, The Origins of Totalitarianism, a very long book, which few people read from start to finish. But the essence of totalitarianism is not hard to understand, it is simply the effort by the state to eliminate all systems of authority except its own, thereby limiting the opportunity for divergent views, which might foster rebellion. Nazi Germany became the model for most of these studies followed closely by Stalin's Soviet Union. Arendt unfortunately did not live long enough to see the Soviet system collapse from the weight of its own inept bureaucracy and the emergence of all kinds of rebellion.

The lesson that Arendt had already figured out, however, was that the healthy state would encourage the development of autonomous individuals and diverse systems of authority. It needs people to examine each system from a position of love and empathy and rebel accordingly, watering the "tree of liberty" not with their blood but with their understanding as autonomous individuals about what needs to be done to encourage tolerance, love, and empathy in themselves and others and how to adjust the system accordingly.

Nowhere was this possibility for heroic behavior based on love and empathy better demonstrated than in the French village of La Chambon during the Nazi occupation in World War II. The little French village had a unique history stemming from its Hugenot protestant background and the oppression that their ancestors had suffered during the persecution of the Huguenots in the seventeenth century. The experience had made the community especially receptive to the plight of the Jews under the Nazis. Unlike most French villages that collaborated with the Nazis, the villagers of La Chambon determined that they would fight the persecution of the Jews with "weapons of the spirit". Using the medieval tradition of sanctuary, the village gave refuge to thousands of Jews who passed through the village in their attempt to escape Nazi persecution. Under the leadership of their pastor, the villagers were united in this effort and none broke ranks to collaborate and report the subterfuge to the Nazis. The villagers themselves when questioned after the war saw nothing unusual in their behavior. They had merely followed their values as interpreted by their spiritual leaders and their own generous instincts and did what they could to right an obvious injustice. Yet, this injustice was as obvious to the French Catholic majority who collaborated with the Nazis as it was to the villagers of La Chambon. Clearly the difference between the two lies in the ability to identify with a persecuted minority and act, not as isolated individuals who themselves would be subject to persecution, but as a committed community acting with solidarity in the interests of a common humanity and responding to laws that were larger than those passed by the state but are universal to the human community.

When the documentary based on the experiences of the people of La Chambon, entitled *Weapons of the Spirit*, was shown to the annual meeting of the American Psychiatric Association, it was given a standing ovation. The gathering was moved by this clear expression of good mental health and the demonstration of the impact of such healthy responses on human history. If the world were composed of villages like La Chambon, there would never be any Nazi occupations.

And, this is my new approach—having thrown off the angry rebellion of old and the depression that went with it, I now merely try to adjust the system towards love and empathy as an expression of my autonomy, and to convince as many of my fellow humans as possible that the solidarity of La Chambon can be recreated in any community based on love and empathy.

Chapter Eight

Depression and Creativity

Writers, along with other creative people, have long been associated with mental illness; the association between genius and madness goes back to at least Aristotle's time. Aristotle noted that "No great genius was without a mixture of genius and melancholia." The Romans considered genius hereditary along with mental illness. The lists of great men who suffered from mental illness is endless and includes a diversity of fields—including the scientist Isaac Newton, the artist Michelangelo, the musician Handel and such politicians as Lincoln and Churchill. The list of artists and writers that have taken the ultimate step to relieve their "melancholia" and committed suicide is long. It includes some of the most renowned and talented representatives of the creative arts; such as, Hart Crane, Vincent Van Gogh, Virginia Wolf, Romain Gary, Sylvia Plath, John Berryman, Jack London, Ernest Hemingway, Sergei Esenin, Vladimir Mayakovsky, and an untold number who like Albert Camus placed themselves in dangerous situations but whose official cause of death is listed as accidental. Among the latter are a substantial number of writers, like the poet, Dylan Thomas, whose lives were shortened by the abuse of alcohol and other drugs and succumbed finally to various afflictions related to lifetimes spent catering to self-destructive addictions.

Despite this impressive historical record, it wasn't until fairly recently that the first significant research on the association between the creative personality and mental illness was produced by Dr. Nancy Andreasen. Using writers from the prestigious Iowa Writers' Workshop, her explorations revealed that writers and their family members suffer a substantially higher rate of mental illness than what could be considered normal. Depression and hypomania were the distinguishing illnesses among the writers, a conclusion that would seem predictable from the anecdotal evidence earlier writers have left behind.

A more detailed study of artists and writers was done in Britain by Dr. Kay Redfield Jamison. As in the earlier study, high rates of mood disorders were found (except among biographers who for some unknown reason—perhaps because they worked with subject matter that related to someone else and their work required less creativity—they were spared the mood swings that were typical of the others). The reported mood swings were related to periods of intensive, highly creative bursts of productivity, near "hypomanic" episodes that were considered essential for the completion of their creative works with peak periods occurring in the spring and fall—an effect that may be related to SAD or Seasonal Affective Disorder. The idea being that those who are subject to SAD would experience such intense energy in the summer, they would be unable to remain sitting long enough to do their writing during the long daylight hours. Winter would bring light deprivation and near-paralyzing depression. That leaves only the spring and fall for creative work As with depression, so with bi-polar disorders like SAD, the trick is to have a mild enough dose to induce creativity. Both severe depression and mania are crippling. Researchers at Harvard University have found that although manic-depressives show a high rate of creativity, their relatives were found to score even higher on creativity tests—these were people who presumably had the same genetic makeup as their bi-polar disordered relatives, but experienced only mild or no detectable mood swings. A little mania can generate ideas and a mild depression can aid critical evaluation, so those who are genetically predisposed to experience mild mood swings may have been better able to survive when creative responses were dictated by changes in the environment, thus successfully passing their genes along and explaining why so many of us are subject to mood swings. For those of us for whom these mood swings cause pain as well as contributing to our creativity and powers of analysis, there are available a wide variety treatment possibilities. It is no longer necessary or wise to resort to alcohol. Lithium is available to manic-depressives; special lighting devices can remedy the pain of winter for those subject to SAD. Prozac and a wide variety of other anti-depressives can relieve depression. How much these drugs decrease creativity while reducing the pain is not known. Because of their concern over the possible loss of creative energy, some people will not use these readily available painkillers. Abbie Hoffman, for example, refused to take lithium because it reduced his energy. Shortly before his suicide he was experimenting with Prozac but never gave it time to take effect. In my own case, the anti-depressant, Nardil, a mao inhibitor, seemed to help in both pushing me out of depression and spurring my creativity. Stopping the drug does not induce depression but the flow of creativity lessens. I am able to sit and consolidate some the work that I did on Nardil, but not much that is new seems to flow. While the experience of depression brings some insight and clarity to the use of my critical faculties, bad depression kills my creativity. For me, recovery tends to bring creativity with it, the desire to tell the world what I have learned is irrepressible. Some of our more famous writers were similarly motivated; Scott Fitzgerald, Joan Didion, and William Styron; all published their experiences in the recovery phase from alcoholism, depression and drug addiction. In a way the recovery phase is much like the first flush of a new romance. The feelings of joy and well being are less focused and may be attributed to anti-depressants, but there is much that is similar. Except that to be really happy, as in the honeymoon stage of a romance, is to be mostly non-creative unless one is a writer of romantic poetry or prose, and, even then, one is likely to create mush rather than inspired literature. The all-consuming demands of love keep one away from the typewriter and the mundane tasks required by good writing. It is like the summer phase of those afflicted with SAD, the abundant sunshine stimulates physical activity not mental gymnastics. To sit indoors and do the solitary creative act is virtually impossible, unless one is aided by an artificial depressant like alcohol—which is what the Cap Cod literary set seems to rely on—writing in the morning, tennis and swimming in the afternoon and booze at night. A little booze could depress the writer enough to allow him to sit still and write—even if he were in love. But, as with using booze to treat depression, using alcohol to curb the excesses of summer joy and/or romance sets up a dangerous precedent—addiction and dependency always are lurking around the corner. For writers, this has been an occupational hazard. A lot of ink has been spilled on the drinking habits of American writers. The affinity for alcohol and other drugs that is found among some of our most famous writers is responsible for a large part of that literature.

Two recent books cover most of the territory. The lives of the most famous of the alcoholic writers has been analyzed from a psychiatric point of view in Donald Goodwin's, *Alcohol and the Writer*, and from a literary—biographical angle in Professor Tom Dardis' new book, *The Thirsty Muse*. Of the two, Goodwin has done far more analysis about the extent to which writers' succumb to alcoholism and the reasons for that happening. He calls it an epidemic involving mainly, although not exclusively, American writers in the first half of the twentieth century. Seventy percent of the American writers who won the Nobel Prize were alcoholics. Thirty percent of the writers in a study done at the University of Iowa's writers' school showed alcoholic traits (a large percentage considering the young age of the majority of those included in the study).

The rest of the evidence is anecdotal but still persuasive—large numbers of known heavy drinkers among writers, tales of alcoholic behavior both in the writing produced and the biographies of the writers, especially of those who came of age in the twenties and thirties. It is hard to ignore the evidence. For the contemporary period, things are less clear, drugs, pills and caffeine, and other alcohol substitutes muddy the waters somewhat, but the inclination for writers to seek both stimulus and escape through addictive substances is a matter of record.

As to why writers seem to be so self indulgent, Goodwin's work is quite clear; the writer has the time to drink without being observed, he is expected to drink, and drinking provides inspiration, confidence to start writing. and a method of stopping the creative wheels once they start spinning. He presents the biographical material of a number of great writers who were clearly alcoholic and reviews the ongoing debate as to whether alcohol inspires writing. Faulkner , for example, certainly thought it did and kept a glass of sipping whiskey by his typewriter. There is a general agreement that had Faulkner been sober, what he produced would have been different if not better. William Styron used alcohol both to treat his depression and to foster the kind of reveries, which he saw as the source of much his creativity. The contemporary screenwriter Oliver Stone makes a similar claim for drugs he took during the war in Vietnam and after; these drugs, he said, freed his mind, liberated his creative potential and allowed him to embark on the career which resulted in the writing of three major movies. Hemingway linked creativity and masculinity with the ability to drink large quantities of liquor—thus setting the standard for masculine self-destruction among writers.

Dardis quotes others who felt they needed to drink to write, frequently using the lubricant analogy—oiling the transmission belt from mind to pen, opening windows to the soul, liberate the mind, break away the rust of everyday life, etc.. It is hard to say how many writers really believed that booze helped them write, the Faulkner syndrome; or, how many used the myth to rationalize their habit. Most writers wrote without drinking during some of their career and most were aware of great writers, like Tolstoy and practically all female writers, who were virtual teetotalers. No writer familiar with the lives of Fitzgerald, Hemingway, or O'Neill could have remained unaware that heavy drinking ultimately extracts its payment in the form of reduced quality and/or quantity. Every age seemed to have its prominent, drink-destroyed, has-been writer. To drink in the face of that record reveals some form of self-destructive urge, usually depression, at work.

The ultimate effect of alcoholism varied with the individual writer. Some like John Cheever have recovered from their bouts with alcoholism and went on to extend their writing careers. Others like John Berryman, Jack London and Ernest Hemingway ultimately succumbed to the combination of alcoholism and depression and committed suicide. Some like William Faulkner, F. Scott Fitzgerald, Sinclair Lewis, Truman Capote, James Agee, and a host of others had their productive lives shortened and the quality of their literary output reduced because of abuse of alcohol and other drugs.

While, a number of American writers were influenced by the macho drinking styles of Jack London and Ernest Hemingway, a slightly different although ultimately just as destructive attitude towards drinking prevailed in the more snobbish literary circles in Britain and America where alcohol consumption was encouraged by the University cultural environment. The biographies and the novels of academia are filled with hard- drinking professors of literature. According to his biographer, even stuffy conservatives like C.S. Lewis were given to excessive consumption at periodic meetings with his students. Kingesley Amis, Britain's prototypical

"Angry Young Man" turned out to be by his own admission, "one of the great drinkers" while winding up his career in both British and American Universities. In his autobiography, Amis credits author Brenda Behan with an "all- round interest in alcohol" and R.P. Blackmur as a "shifter of enough bourbon for two quite thirsty men." Cheever claimed that one of the university's primary functions was to teach undergraduates how to drink. As part of his training, he downed a glass of whiskey every morning before breakfast. Here in the university setting, in a protected environment far from the rugged settings described by Hemingway, London and Steinback, literary prima donnas use alcohol not so much as a manly outlet for relaxation, but as a lubricant for high-sounding discourse. For most, drinking bouts in the university were an easy way to test their alcoholic consumption capacities; but for the susceptible, like Lewis, Fitzgerald, Cheever, and Styron. It was the beginning of an addictive slide into oblivion.

Writing for a living provides both the opportunity and some incentive to drink. That the addictive personality will succumb under those conditions seems to be the mechanism that ensnares so many writers. For the purpose of consistency, our working definition is that an addiction seems to exist when a person's attachment to a sensation, object, or another person is such to lessen his appreciation for and ability to deal with other things in his environment, so that he has become increasingly dependent on that experience as his only source of gratification. A healthy person chooses the time and conditions under which he will drink and uses alcohol only to enhance other activities in his life that are important to him. The addictive person's weakness is that he cannot choose when and how much to drink or to love—he drinks or loves to the exclusion of those other things in his life that give him a sense of identity. An addictive person can switch his addiction from booze to Jesus, to heroin, to sex, ad infinitum. Fitzgerald, for example, alternated between his consuming attachment to Sheilla Graham, to boozing, to Caffeine and Coca Cola.

Of the great writers, his is the clearest example of the addictive personality that we have. The addictive personality is usually the psychological reflection of some kind of thwarted development; the single sourcing aspect of addiction is infantile in nature reflecting a basic insecurity about the consistency of maternal affection. The dependability of alcohol and other drugs is a large part of its attraction for these tortured souls. Unlike their mothers or wives, alcohol is always there. All the writers studied by Dardis and Goodwin continued to drink well beyond the point where it was arguable whether or not alcohol was accomplishing its appointed task of promoting their creativity.

None of these great writers succeeded in regulating their intake to the precise amount of alcohol needed to maintain their writing. Eventually the alcohol came to control them and became the main focus of their lives. Hence they passed the criteria for addiction, as their devotion to alcohol swallowed up their drive to write. Faulkner tried valiantly to control his drinking to the point of hiring a man to feed him precise quantities of whiskey at intervals he decided would allow him to function while satisfying his body's craving for alcohol. But even this did not succeed, and he inevitably would stumble into binge drinking. Most reached the point where the only important thing in their life was where their next drink was coming from.

Eugene O'Neil is one of the very few writers who were able to overcome his alcoholism (leaving aside the technical question of where just heavy drinking becomes alcoholism) through sheer will power and went on to do his best writing during his period of complete sobriety. During this time, his inspiration is clearly from the desire to get the story of his disease into artistic form. The result, *Long Day's Journey into the Night*, stands as one of the great plays of the twentieth century and certainly the greatest literary analysis of the alcoholic family that we have.

It is certainly unfortunate that it is the charismatic alcoholics who influence the succeeding generation and not the example provided by O'Neil. Hemingway was perhaps the most charismatic of them all and holds the record for dragging others into his alcoholic wake. His relationship with Fitzgerald was based on his alcoholic leadership qualities. Able to hold prodigious quantities himself, he openly associated drink with manliness and held Fitzgerald in contempt because he could not keep up. For years, Hemingway's reputation was built on a presumed ability to drink all night and arise to write early each morning. Later biographers have raised questions about this view of the man and have shown that drinking incapacitated him on occasion as it does everyone else; he often slept late after drinking bouts and wrote little or nothing on those days.

No doubt the loneliness of the professional writer who spends his working day looking inward and sometimes uses alcohol to aid in the process, makes him receptive to the instant feelings of companionship provided by the basic ingredients of most bars, alcohol and conversation. Many of the best writers were also great storytellers or at least loved to be around the raconteurs who frequent bars and provide the stories that find their way into novels. All this can be justified in the name of research; either gathering material or trying material out on a receptive audience. While the basic biographical features of the famous writers' descent into alcoholism are a matter of record, some aspects of the problem are not. For example, the extent to which depression figures into the writer's addiction is far less clear.

Alcoholism in its classic form is fairly well understood, but the relationship between alcohol, depression and creativity is not. As Goodwin points out, it is virtually impossible to figure out what psychological problem is plaguing a drunk until the alcohol is out of his system. Most of these writers never got the alcohol out of their systems long enough for an analysis to be made (Styron is the notable exception here and his book, *Darkness Visible*, on his conquest of depression and alcohol abuse is an inspiration for all writers threatened by both or either). The treatment for alcoholism is different from that of depression even though there are some similarities. As we pointed out in Chapter Two, the typical Alcoholic Anonymous twelve step program will work fine on many alcoholics, but something further is needed to treat the depression, which motivates much excessive drinking. We are familiar with a wide range of anti-depressants, which when combined with therapy usually will cure the minor depression that many of us suffer from. But for the anti-depressants to work, alcohol consumption has to be controlled before the slow process of rebuilding the life styles of the addictive-depressive personality can begin.

The life style demanded by writing for a living is by its very nature a lonely and depressing vocation. The writer works alone. He looks deeply into his own nature and the society he lives in. For the sensitive, unhappy young person the process of writing can be both a source of comfort and addictive-escapist vehicle. It may be easier for him to write about life than to experience it. The short-term rewards of writing are few. A compulsion for creative expression is almost a necessity given the long span between writing the first novel and public recognition, if it ever comes. Some satisfaction has to be derived from the process itself, or the writer will turn to endeavors in which he can earn a living more easily. The competition for a limited market for creative fiction and non-fiction is fierce. Unless he is lucky enough to write an immediate best seller, almost all other professions are far more rewarding. Once published he faces unrelenting criticism. His chances for future publication are uncertain.

To endure in the face of all these negative aspects requires an enormous sense of self and the willingness to sacrifice for the sake of a self-fulfillment based upon doing what is important to one's self, for the hope of immortality or whatever else is motivating the writer. Most fail and disappointment and depression usually come with failure. Most of the alcoholic writers were given to depressive self-flagellation even in their own creations. Malcolme Lowrey's, *Under the Volcano*, which is generally conceded to be our best alcoholic novel is ridden with perceptive self degradation as the novel's hero watches himself sink ever deeper into destructive behavior. An alcoholic himself, Lowrey had personally endured much of what he was writing about.

Similar accounts can be found in Fitzgerald's *Crack-Up*, London's *John Barleycorn*, and several of the late novels and stories by John Cheever and Phillip Roth. A depressed writer has called the last of John Updike's popular "Rabbit" books." Albert Camus' famous work, The Fall, is a classic piece notable for its semi-autobiographical description of a man who like Camus himself was suffering from severe depression.

The irony and the tragedy of these cases is that the awareness demonstrated by the creative writer in his work rarely translates into effective action to promote his own well being. The process seems to be similar in each case. The good writer is aware of his own weaknesses, and sometimes describes them brilliantly through his characters, but usually stops short of resolving the dynamic behind the depressive behavior, for himself or his fictitious character. Amis's *Lucky Jim* manages to stay semi-pickled most of the time like the author who created him. Even when forced to go "cold turkey" after being hospitalized for a broken leg, Amis refuses to recognize the significance of his hallucinations an "a touch of madness" with the withdrawal of alcohol. And, when a doctor recommends he at least keep track of his consumption he asks, "To what end?" In this Amis follows the normal alcoholic response of ignoring and denying the symptoms which if unheeded lead to his own destruction.

For the depressive-alcoholic writer, resolving his problem would require an effort of the magnitude made by only a few like O'Neil and Styron who quit drinking and went into therapy. Most alcoholic writers were too firmly committed to denying their booze problem except as it appears in their writing. While writing can be a form of therapy, it does not by itself offer a cure. O'Neil, for example, wrote our most perceptive account of the addictive family, but fell back into alcoholism towards the end of his life. His reason may have seen the problem but he never worked out the emotional source of his addictive behavior.

Although their are variations in background and lifestyle among these writers, what they all seem to have in common is a sensitivity to the world around them combined with an inability to relate well to other humans. This difficulty is exhibited by multiple marriages in the case of Hemingway, Steinback, and Lowrey, by long tragic relationships with O'Neil and Fitzgerald, and unhappy bachelorhoods for Faulkner, C.S. Lewis, and Truman Capote.

Despite their brilliance in the field of creative writing none of these great men showed much creativity in working out their relationship problems. Most looked for women who would tolerate their addictions and live in their shadow. Hemingway died locked into a macho view of women and the world. Sensitive to the follies of the world, they blamed their personal troubles on those around them.

Fitzgerald turned on his ex-lover with surprising vindictiveness when she would not return to their destructive relationship. Capote's last book was an indictment of many of his personal friends, as was much of the autobiography of Kingsley Amis. While capable of showing a remarkable understanding of themselves and the world, they seemed incapable of using this knowledge to good effect in their personal lives. A lot of their failure in relationships is explained by their descent into alcohol addiction. For many it was a substitute for the lack of good relationships.

As writer Dan Wakefield, explained in a recent issue of

Longevity magazine, booze was a replacement for a sheltering, over-protective mother drowning out difficult issues that he had never been expected to face. Wakefield is one of the very few writers to deal with the childhood roots of his own drinking problems and even take the significant step of criticizing his parents. Wakefield also used alcohol to help break down his inhibitions against the expression of feelings and then went through the classic addictive dependency syndrome—the more dependent and addictive the drinking became the more estranged he became. Fortunately for Wakefield, the threat of death was enough to motivate him to do something about his addiction and he began the long process to sobriety and health.

At the bottom in the throes of addiction, the writer can separate himself not only from people but from his own creations as well. Towards the end of his life, William Faulkner often did not even remember what he had written, having been drunk during its writing, so even if it contained great perceptions, it did him no good. Malcolme Lowry, who, it is generally conceded, has written the greatest alcoholic novel, continued to drink himself into the grave just as the hero of masterpiece, *Under the Volcano*, did. Truman Capote wrote our most psychologically perceptive novel about his childhood but was unable to turn those understandings into the personal growth necessary to save him from alcoholism and drug addiction. Albert Camus could write brilliantly about depression and alienation but could not deal with his own depressive nature.

It was as though these writers could face themselves only in the creative writing process and could not face themselves in relationship to other humans. Lacking the skills to relate easily they turned to booze and writing as their only sources of easing the pain they found in themselves and the world and most were never able to break out of the addictive lifestyles they developed.

To a man, they were unable to switch from the creative, lonely work they were involved in to other, potentially healthier avenues of employment such as journalistic work that involves more contact with people. This has been the route taken by Tom Wolfe and Norman Mailer, who together have pioneered the "new journalism" which combines the art of the novelist with the reporting abilities of the good journalist. They both have avoided alcoholism.

According to Alice Miller, the author of several books on child abuse, a major portion of the psychological damage done to children, stems from the repression of the need of healthy children to discharge legitimate feelings. Obedience is demanded and individual preference is suppressed. They cannot express anger at their parents or teachers. Instead they must repress or deny their feelings; the result can be depression, addiction and even suicide. Miller uses the suicide of the poet Sylvia Plath to illustrate her point. Plath's suicide according to Miller was based on the false life she felt forced to live because of pressure from her mother. She also points out that that literature is one of the most acceptable and profitable forms for the release of these pent up emotions. It is safe because all forms of reproaches can be placed in the mouths of fictitious characters. While Plath was able to release some of her feelings through her poetry, it was apparently insufficient to prevent her from taking her own life. Right up until her death, she was apparently lying to her mother about how her life was going. Her suicide can be seen as one of the few truly authentic actions that she had ever taken—the ultimate act which at once proclaimed both her pain and her autonomy, her final and only significant act of rebellion.

This may be the psychological key that explains much of the destructive drinking that is done by writers. Seeing clearly through their writing the necessity for change in the society around them, they are unable to overcome parental and societal prohibitions against rebellion. Their only rebellion comes through their writings that has the effect of increasing their dissatisfaction without the kinds of releases that active rebellion would have. Hence, the need to drink to overcome the feelings of alienation brought on by their own creations. They have rebelled only in internal way as the act of creation is by its nature an act of rebellion against the status quo—the writer changes life by the application of his creative skills to the reality he sees. But as the psychologist Arno Gruen has pointed out, rebellion alone will not make a human being.

To really fulfill his development in authentic manner he must somehow act on the perceptions he has developed or cause a split between mind and body. To complete this process he must deal with his childhood and come to grip with rebellion against his parents that was so painful for Sylvia Plath. Turning to alcohol instead is a way of dying before death has come so that rebellion can be avoided.

This explains why even among famous and talented writers, biographical data about their childhood is scarce and criticism of their parents even scarcer. Styron's, *Darkness Visible* describes with great perception his own descent into depression and the suicidal impulses that accompanied it, but never probes the childhood roots of his troubles. Plath's autobiography, *The Bell Jar*, is mostly about her college career and the traumas associated with losing her virginity and leaving her parent's but there is no description of her childhood and no potentially lifesaving critique of her mother. So deep are society's messages against violating the Fourth Commandment, it is only rarely that we get a glimpse into the family life of an author that is critical of his parents. Partly, this may be the result of a natural inclination to repress negative thoughts about one's own parents, an inclination that is fostered by the parents while the child is weak and helpless. Hence, any thought of rebelling against parents brings with it those old feelings of being weak and helpless—feelings that are unbearable for most, and which caused Sylvia Plath to commit suicide rather than confront them. Criticism of society and brutal people appear frequently in the great works of out time but mostly outside of the author's family. Truman Capote's work is exceptional in that he has written about himself within a family setting that is both sensitive and critical.

Alice Miller claims that when that kind of profound working through of one's anger at parental oppression does appear in print, it is highly beneficial both to the individual and society. It gives the individual the freedom to act independently, take a stand against all forms of repression and generally keep from repeating the acts of hostility perpetrated on him by his family. The society gains by example of how to attain their autonomy and begin to fight their own histories.

For the writer, the mere process of getting his feelings out on paper can be therapeutic, especially if he is blocked and unable to express them in any other way—which is the case for many writers and is the answer to why they choose writing as a vocation in the face of almost overwhelming odds against their possible success. The personal act of intellectual rebellion it takes to capture and change reality on paper can translate into action in the world.

Many of the writers, especially those in the Hemingway,

Steinback, London era, took stands against oppression and acted upon their beliefs, taking part in the Spanish Civil War, and supporting rights for workers and Blacks. They seemed unable, however, to take the next step and do the sort of self analysis that might have allowed them to recognize the dynamics behind their depressive alcoholic behavior. Trying to save the world seemed appropriate while the awareness necessary to save themselves seemed beyond them. They seemed to transfer the causes of their own unhappiness on to society, making legitimate criticisms and often acting upon them in a heroic fashion, but, unfortunately, to a man, they also ignored the childhood roots of their own unhappiness. To admit to those roots would bring back too many feelings of helplessness—a difficult thing to face for most of us, but almost impossible for those imbued with the Hemingway brand of machoism. We are left, then, with great writing and sometimes heroic actions but psychologically destructive and childish behavior.

The authentic feeling, realistically captured is a powerful art form, which is why almost all of the best writing is autobiographical in its roots. If that authentic expression is rewarded by the praise of those the author respects the resulting high is one of life's sweetest pleasures, but if it is rejected; the pain is correspondingly intense. The closer to the author's own life the work is, the more intense the feelings that go with the rejection. Since the market place dictates more rejection than acceptance, there being far more submissions than could ever possibly be published, the writer has to be prepared for pain even if his writing is outstandingly creative. The lonely existence of the writer means that he does not have the usual disappointment-relieving mechanisms most of us have built into our jobs where sympathetic fellow workers stand ready to of solace.

Working alone with no one else familiar with the work he has created the writer must bear his disappointment alone. Turning inward, he may spin down into depression. The same turning inward that may either induce further productive creativity or it may bring him down into despair. Individuals differ in their capacity to handle rejection, but, as we have seen, writers tend to be an especially sensitive group.

Which may be part of the reason why some of the alcoholic authors discussed above were afflicted with not just the every day mildly depressed state that many of us suffer from. They became depressed to the point that institutional commitment was their only hope. Like Hemingway, who was clearly treating his depression with alcohol, they reached a point in their downward cycle where alcohol no longer relieved the pain and ended up as suicides. Some, like Faulkner, seemed to be aware that the booze was killing them but were unable to limit their intake to just that amount which had fueled their creativity and kept depression at bay.

Only a very few of these, like John Cheever, who were both alcoholic and showed depressive tendencies and; most recently, William Styron, were able to quit drinking in time to extend their productive lives. Most freely admitted they drank to dull the pain of living. Truman Capote claimed it was his superior intellect that made him so sensitive and Malcolme Cowley claimed "that it was like he had been born without a skin." Almost all showed their sensitivity and heightened awareness of the human condition. This as we have come to expect as the hallmark of the great writer. All were aware of their own mortality and some obsessed with it. Hemingway did battle with a mystical "giant", London with a John Barleycorn pressing him towards death. Some saw death as an attractive escape. Sylvia Plath found it her most significant, authentic act finally putting together her feelings and behavior someplace other than only in her poems.

There seems to be a way in which depression, like alcohol, aids the creative process, although none of the writers mentioned above seemed aware of the process. Recent studies indicate that the depressed person tends to evaluate his own situation and his environment more realistically than so-called "normal" people who tend to hold strongly to optimistic illusions about themselves and the world. The depressed writer would, then, present us with a clearer picture of reality. He may indeed be driven to write to relieve the burden of the suffering he sees around him and inside himself. Hence, Steinback was able to record the oppression of the Okies and the painful exodus to California in the 1930's. Fitzgerald makes us aware of the pain endured by the great Gatsby, and Capote is able to capture the suffering of his own childhood.

For these writers, depression turned their thoughts inward and alcohol seemed necessary to ease the pain of their own understanding while they transmitted their reality to the printed page. To stare steadily into the darkness of the human condition, alone and aided only by the drive to achieve a certain degree of immortality through one's creations, demands great courage. As Goodwin notes, to have the hubris to place your perceptions out in front of the critics is part of what it takes to be a writer. A good writer must not only be inspired but must act as his own critic taking the un-formulated inspiration and turning it into an art form that transmits his message. if his writing is at all autobiographical, then he is acting as a critic of himself and belaboring his own imperfections.

For the sensitive writer, this process may easily become obsessive. The writer who is a perfectionist, as Malcolme Lowrey was, may drive himself into a cycle of endless corrections that never allow him to finish his work—as Lowry's only published novels had to be literally torn from his hands. Alcohol seems to make this syndrome worse as the disease progresses. The alcoholic writer seems to able to recognize his imperfections but is unable to keep enough of the complete work in his alcohol-bemused mind to bring the work to a satisfactory conclusion.

Given all of this, who can blame the depressed writer if he turns for comfort to the most readily available and most socially acceptable of drugs to ease the pain of his own perceptions and the scorn of critics who don't understand or understand all too clearly? The irony of his situation is that the depressed condition that causes him to see clearly into himself and the human environment and which helps him create works of genius also causes him overwhelming pain which drives him to drink. If there were a way he could control his depression, limit his drinking to the precise amount required to treat his depression and fuel his creativity, all the while continuing to live the solitary life of the professional writer, it would be a balancing act that would require a rare sense of self that is uncommon, especially among those sensitive souls who are attracted to the writing profession.

This is not to say that all writers suffer from depression. Tom Wolfe, the acclaimed writer of *Bonfire of the Vanities*, *The Right Stuff*, and the *Electric Kool Aid Acid Test*, for example, seems not to need either depression or excessive amounts of alcohol to fuel his creativity. His work penetrates and critiques a wide variety of American social scenes with wit, magnificent, descriptive talent, and cutting satire, but never the kind of morbid self examination that one finds in the depressed writer. It is hard to imagine Wolfe writing a self-critical autobiographical work like Fitzgerald's *Crack-Up*, or Joan Didion's self portrait in *The White Album*. And, not having suffered like William Styron, Wolfe could not match Styron's, *Memoir of Madness*.

Styron's work in fact gives us the best example available of the crucial relationship of depression and alcohol. Forced to quit drinking because of a metabolic change that made him unable to tolerate alcohol, he felt "emotionally naked" and "vulnerable". Depression gripped him and without the alcohol to relieve his sadness, he became unable to write. Like Cheever before him, Styron was able to get treatment before he acted on his suicidal impulses. It remains to be seen if he can, as have Cheever and O'Neil, regain his creative genius now that he seems to have overcome both his drinking and his depression Styron's case offers an interesting alternative to the Faulknerian theory that booze feeds the bard. When Styron was forced to quit drinking, he could still write. It was only when his depression set in that he became paralyzed and could not write. Both Cheever and O'Neil remained productive after quitting drinking, but, although both seemed to be unhappy, neither was afflicted with the kind of crippling depression that gripped Styron. Driven to hospitalization by his suicidal impulses, Styron describes his depression more vividly than any other author has done. He even links part of his depressive tendencies to his parents, but falls short of the critical approach that would have lifted his book into the ranks of a singular masterpiece. In the end he mourns his mother but does not separate from her and gives her credit for rescuing him from suicide through the music that he had heard her sing. Alcohol may be of some use to the depressed writer who is seeking to keep his depression at bay sufficiently to allow him to write. In Styron's case that seems to be true because it is only after he stops drinking that the awareness of his depression settles in. Styron was fortunate that a physical intolerance for alcohol forced him to stop drinking before his use of alcohol to fight depression had made sobriety intolerable forcing him to seek a constant supply to avoid confronting this intolerable pain. When the alcoholic hits bottom and is forced to confront his situation, suicide may seem the easiest way out.

Styron was saved by his own body from following the route chosen by Hemingway, London, Berryman and a host of others.

Because of the more sensational aspects of their alcohol consumption and resultant suicide, the problems of these authors with depression have not been given proper attention. The importance of Styron's case is that his depression continued and grew worse after he quit drinking so he was forced to focus on his depression, not his drinking. He then could turn to treatment for the depression without the crippling attachment to alcohol that had caused so many before him to commit suicide. Not that he was not suicidal—he was that—but he was sober enough to realize that he could be helped and that he could live without alcohol. For the others, the choice of life without alcohol was one that would require a tremendous act of courage since they knew only the pain that accompanied sobriety and had no awareness that it might be possible for them to reap the joy implicit in a life of sobriety unaccompanied by depression (one of the more unfortunate aspects of the literature of sobriety is that it tends to stress duty and a goody-two-shoe morality that makes most intelligent, cynical drunks, as writers tend to be, gag and reach for another drink).

I know my own attempts to arrive at an understanding of my particular pattern of creativity and the relationship between it and depression and my own flirtation with alcoholism has been difficult. A long struggle to get and stay sober was necessary before I arrived at any significant understanding of the forces driving me to drink and causing my depression. Drawing a graph of my depressions was quite easy. Those followed clear time lines based mostly on the state of my primary relationship. I could quite clearly draw four major peaks and troughs based on three failed marriages and three major primary, although unmarried relationships. Since I had no strong secondary relationships and was dependent on these primary relationships for my sense of well being, the decline of that primary relationship always triggered a depression. But my creative pattern was far less clear. I also seemed to have a slight case of SAD, with spurts of productivity coming in the spring and a tendency to break up relationships in the depths of winter. I never was clinically depressed and always managed some creative expression even at my worst. My most productive periods, however, seemed to follow on the heels of my romantic interludes. Once I got over the puppy love stage, the psychic energy created by the romance usually, but not always, seemed to stir my creative juices. The flow was especially pronounced when the relationship turned the corner and headed down. Then I would turn inward and what was inside would get written down. How much creativity resulted seemed unrelated to how much the relationship aroused my passions. On the other hand as my relationship ended and the depression got bad, my creativity, was lost along with the relationship.

Also, there seemed to be some relationship between my creative moments and the anti-depressants I was taking. The creativity tended to pick up again as the medicine took hold. For the last four years, I have been trying to build the basic ingredients of an un-depressed life style. I have improved my relationships with most people by increasing my awareness of their emotions and demonstrating that understanding along with a clearer expression of my own. One readily, demonstrably-positive result has been almost eight years of un-interrupted employment—a record for me. In the past when plagued by depression and my own attempts to treat it with alcohol, I rarely kept a job for more than a year, and often was unemployed or only employed part-time. This ability to relate better to people has taken some of the anxiety-creating burden of placing all of the responsibility for my sense of well being on one relationship. That has allowed me to place a different value on what I create. Money, fame, and immortality no longer motivate me with the same intensity. My primary concerns are now with personal relationships, mental and physical health, and the development of skills related to those areas.

One by-product of this new attitude is that I have decided it is not worth becoming depressed or alcoholic just to spur my creative production. I am willing to learn from the writing styles of the writers discussed above, but I intend to avoid their addictive life styles.

The other major lesson, stressed by every teacher from Freud to Alice Miller, is the importance of separation (or rebellion) from parental influences that feed the addictive-depressive personality. I have captured some of this in my writing and am trying to complete the psychological break that will allow the full autonomy or identity that can finally liberate me from those patterns of behavior I learned as child and have so plagued my adult life.

Chapter Nine

Depression and Religion

Perhaps no phrase in human history has been more misunderstood than Karl Marx's famous declaration that "religion is the opiate of the people." The common assumption has been that the atheist Marx was arrogantly dismissing religion as just another drug which the masses used to endure life; numbing them so that they would not fight for what was justly their inheritance—the product of their labor which was being stolen from them by the ruling classes. This interpretation has lasted because it has some truth. Marx and his followers did see some of this in the way religion was used historically. But, for Marx, the role of religion was far more complicated. He often talked about religion as representing some of the most worthy aspirations of human life. For Marx, the tragedy of most religions was that they placed their rewards beyond life; happiness, love, leisure—all came only after death and then only to those who followed rules set by church leaders. What Marx wanted to do was to place all of these within the grasp of mortals while they were alive, to place the best of human aspirations within the realm of the obtainable for everyone.

The other key concept that is implied in the term opiate is the concept of religion as a tool of social control; the equating of rebellion and sin by entwining church and state and making rebellion against the state a sin. It then acts as inhibitor of revolt. Even in America where there was a theoretical separation between church and state, the church stood as a barrier against social upheaval. Marx understood this but his main concern was with the principle of delayed gratification—especially when that delay meant never on earth. The church used the concept of delayed gratification to create discipline in its followers—sex was delayed until after marriage, thriftiness equated with Godliness, idleness the work of the devil. All these teachings reinforced the doctrines that were being imposed in the work place. The spread of religion to the workers had the effect of bringing middle class, or capitalist, values to the workers. Not all workers, of course, for there never were enough churches to accommodate any but a small percentage of the workers.

Social control was achieved through the concept of sin. Salvation through grace was obtainable only through the church. Judgements about who was or was not in a state of grace and hence saved was made by the church leadership. The rules of conduct and the signs of grace were clear. Prosperity was a clear indication that God was pleased. Industry and sobriety were both evidence of grace and the means of obtaining such. Those who were not prosperous, industrious and sober must be in a state of sin.

Sex also played a special role for lust was something that was always a matter of concern for most men. The Christian home was kept as sexless as possible to avoid arousing lustful thoughts. Sex was merely for procreation—never for recreation.

Masturbation was among the worst of sins and since most boys either masturbated on occasion or at least wanted to, the church had a ready made sin to make all feel guilty. Everyone was a potential sinner—males by yielding to lustful thoughts and females because they inspired lust and hence sin. Sexual energy could only be safely sublimated into one's work or through church sponsored festivals.

Schoolteachers and parents spread the same doctrine as the ministers so that the control mechanisms were virtually totalitarian for the children who had religious parents. Alice Miller has looked at this system as it grew in Germany and has condemned it for fostering the kind of environment that led to the growth of fascism. The key reason for that according to Miller was that there was no room for the development of independent judgment. Children were subject to authoritarian and brutal conditioning designed to create obedient workers and citizens—not healthy and happy humans.

During most of the nineteenth century, there was not a great deal of difference between Europe and America in these matters. The variety of religious experiences was somewhat greater in America. Evangelical movements have always found America a more receptive environment for their more extreme doctrines. Liberal religions, Unitarians, Universalists, and Quakers were also more active although much smaller in terms of numbers than the evangelicals. But while theology and spiritual fervor differed, the basic message was similar—hard work, sobriety, and sexual sublimation were the keys to salvation. Democracy was something that occurred in the voting booth but rarely had any effect on the work place, the church, or the school. Miller could just as easily have done her work in America.

What rankled Miller about the use of religion as a tool to create a docile, non-rebellious labors supply was also behind most of Marx's complaints. Man was alienated not only from the products of his labor but also from his vision, to use Scott Peck's term, of what life was all about. What replaced it was a methodology for instilling discipline at the price of his personal integrity and his capacity for independent judgment. Basically it committed him to permanent childhood.

Also, the new religion was schizophrenic in its application. The old Catholicism had taken all aspects of the world under its jurisdiction. The new Protestantism left the world of politics, business, and science outside the scope of its control. The new religion was reduced to cheerleading the business and political worlds, fearfully attacking science and exerting its influence primarily over family life and the educational process. Modern man was left with a vision of the world that was incomplete and based, as Joseph Chamberlain has pointed out, on a myth designed for an ancient Hebrew culture that was far more primitive and in some respects totally at odds with contemporary views, especially about women and slaves.

In spite of this reduction in its influence, religion still has had an enormous influence in creating an environment for unhealthy attitudes, especially about sex and reducing the area where individuals ought to be exercising their spiritual growth through independent judgment.

The capacity for independent judgment is not fostered in America just as it still is not fostered in Germany; the creation of infantile adults dependent on authority is a fact of life in America just as it is in Germany. Only once in recent memory were a large number of Americans raised in relatively permissive circumstances. This was in the post WWII period when the more permissive child raising influenced a segment of American society, largely middle class, advocated by Dr. Benjamin Spock and the parents and doctors around the country who adhered to his doctrines. These children swelled the ranks of the civil rights and anti-war movements of the 1960's. They showed an unusual capacity for independent judgment and became convinced that the values of their parents were lacking. They rejected sexual sublimation, compulsive work, and sobriety—even cleanliness was attacked on the grounds that their parents concern with clean bodies, underarm deodorants and avoiding halitosis caused them to ignore their existence as people. The civil rights movement dramatically displayed the contradiction between the values of freedom and equality that had been given lip service in their school civics courses and the reality of segregation being challenged on television screens in their living rooms. Faced with the possibility of death in a pointless war in Vietnam, delayed gratification made no sense either. Mixing this with a potent cultural stew that emphasized sex, drugs, and rock and roll, the movement grew and ultimately shook the entire nation.

There were some successes that came with the turmoil of the sixties. Legislation was passed changing forever the legal status of Blacks, removing the outward signs of segregation. The war eventually was ended. Unfortunately the revolt did not however change the basis of American cultural life that had created the rebellion. The economic and political system remained intact. The religions that had buttressed that system also remained in their support capacities. The same system that had kept children from developing into adults with the capacity for independent judgment—that kept them attached to their parents and through that attachment to the system that oppressed them—that system remained intact.

Hence, those who were depressed before by the system's attacks on their development continued to be depressed after the excitement of the sixties subsided and the system regained its hold on the psyches of Americans. In fact, for some, those who had developed a vision of a truly free society and convinced themselves that the political activity of the sixties would give that vision a reality, the return of the old bureaucrats led by Nixon and Reagan was too much and they committed some form of suicide. For leaders like singer Phil Ochs and Yippie Abbie Hoffman, taking their own lives seemed the only way to obtain relief. For others, the contrast between the possibilities of the new vision and the reality of the return of the old system was depressing but something that had to be endured.

The system allowed more flexibility after the sixties. Sex, drugs, and rock and roll were still available—they all became more expensive but still were more obtainable than in the fifties. All but the most fundamentalist churches turned a blind eye to premarital sex. Marijuana and heroin was available practically everywhere and rock stars became rich and respectable. Organized religion generally backed off from these areas as it had backed off from proscribing business and political life earlier. It was a small victory towards the development of autonomous adults capable of independent judgments in the area of sex, drugs, and music; or, so it seemed.

Unfortunately, what the system gave with one hand it took with the other. The free sex of the sixties became cramped by the epidemic of Aids in the eighties; the relatively harmless weed, the recreational drug of choice was replaced by high potency and much more addictive products in the eighties; crack replaced heroin and a war on drugs was started. Music was left, but without the war and the freedom movement, the lilting lyrics of the sixties degenerated into hedonism, and it was hard to find anything liberating in the sheer greed and exploitation which became the hallmark of the post 60's music business.

The return of the old virtues of hard work, cleanliness, loyalty and patriotism, this time without their religious dressing, became the dominant feature of the contemporary period. Motivation had little to do with the Godliness by which capitalist grasping was justified before. Sheer unvarnished greed motivated the new Yuppies. Enrollment in business schools mushroomed and liberal arts enrollment declined correspondingly.

Simultaneously, statistics for the number of people seeking help for depression grew each year. With the enlarging of the scope of activity unaddressed by the church or any other value creating organization, the nagging question of why the relentless search for material reward went unanswered. The old answers of upward mobility for the glory of God, family, and country were no longer acceptable but nothing new had replaced those values. Relentless activity simply to provide more consumer goods left most people with a feeling of emptiness. The historian, Christopher Lasch has referred to this syndrome as "The Age Of Narcissism." Like the Greek God, Narcissus, America seemed to exchanging its heritage for the shallow reflection of itself that was being sold on television. Cosmetics and deodorants made things smell and look better but did nothing to change the underlying reality. But, with the aid of television and drugs, that reality could be temporarily ignored.

Also, it became increasing clear to all but the most unobservant that the price for unrestrained consumption may well be the destruction of the planet as a place inhabitable for humans.

The destruction of parts of the ozone layer and the increasing carbon dioxide in the atmosphere with its threat of global warming was facts that few could ignore. The Christian religion was found deficient for it had long placed man in the center of the universe and had encouraged the domination of nature rather than promoting the harmony that American Indian and Asian religions espoused.

Sales of new anti-depressant drugs such as Prozac climbed to all time highs competing for the first time with the profits from alcohol—the poor man's antidepressant. It was becoming clear that parents no longer had answers for basic questions about the meaning of life. The old threats of hellfire and brimstone were no longer believable. Discipline came from the television and assorted computer games. The minds of children were converted into instruments of demand for the products hyped by the companies that purchased the television time. The unfillable gap that came with an upbringing lacking in affectionate nurturing became an enormous advantage for advertisers eager to help children fill the void in their lives with junk foods and plastic trivia. Since the supplies seem endless to parent and child, only alert, concerned and highly motivated parents could fight the wave that engulfed those around them.

Yet, there are those emerging from the onslaught with dignity intact. Those who would look back to Albert Schweitzer for his teachings on the "reverence of life", to Thoreau for the glorification of the simple life, to Ghandi for his implementation of the simplicity and dignity of life in the struggle for freedom, to Martin Buber for his insistence on "I—Thou" relationships and the refusal to be an "it", to Freud for his insistence on proclaiming the importance of Eros, or love, in the struggle against Thanatos, or death, in the relations between humans, and, above all, to Marx for recognizing the proposition that it is here on earth where the finest efforts of man need to be directed and when that happens the alienation of man from his environment and his own psychic being dissolves.

The challenge, then, as Joseph Chamberlain described it shortly before his death, is to create a new myth applicable for our time, as the Old Testament was applicable to ancient Hebrew civilization and the New Testament to Medieval Society. In fact, those of us who went through the struggles of the sixties were creating some of the new values that would go into the new religion. The ideals and vision of equality as expressed in Martin Luther King's famous "I Have A Dream" speech lives on in spite of the death of the man and his movement. The idea of participatory democracy expressed in the Port Huron statement of the Students for a Democratic Society is still remembered by those who tried to give the idea some reality in student communes and in the Free University. The women's liberation movement has remained vital even in the face of an increasingly conservative society and the European Green movement has thrust environmental concerns onto the forefront of politics in most of the major countries across the Atlantic.

Slowly, a consciousness is developing that proclaims the importance of the development of the individual's capacity for independent judgment over the imposition of family authority, that reduces the ability of organized religion to lower self esteem by fostering guilt over the expression of human sexuality, that is making the school's more responsive to the needs of children for opportunities to test and develop their capacity for independent judgment in a safe environment, and to make the political and industrial spheres more sensitive to the ideals of participatory democracy and environmental protection.

What has not been addressed is how to go beyond the development of free and equal individuals to creating new communities based on love and empathy. The extension of love has been a primary goal of most of the world's religions, "Love thy neighbor" has almost always been a hard thing for most people to do. Churches have traditionally used the concept to promote charity. The difficulty with this has always been that if charity is left to the church, the individual's choice and responsibility is taken from him, the I—Thou component is removed, charity becomes something one does through a checkbook, and love is removed. Part of the problem always has been due to that fact that churches have been much more interested in promoting guilt than in extending love. Put together by people who did not love themselves, there was no way they could love their neighbor. Consequently charity was frequently directed far from the point of initiation—missions to Africa and Asia were and still are great favorites. Souls were "saved" and the more immense problem of creating a loving environment at home was avoided.

It was the theoretical equivalent of projecting reward for good works beyond death. Charity carried out half way around the world was no threat to the situation at home. The labor market at home was unspoiled by any handouts. Any idea that the wealthy should share the profits from local industries with the poor at home was nipped in the bud. Discrimination against Blacks at home could continue if the conscious was appeased by the knowledge that Black souls were being saved in Africa.

Churches could not afford to look to closely at their own communities. Their largest contributors were likely to be those who worked for or owned factories and natural resources. References to fair wages and environmental conservation would tread on well-shod feet and the minister knew better than to alienate his biggest contributors. The easiest course was to concentrate on old lessons from the Bible and let the problems art home fester. Hence, most churches are virtually irrelevant to the community problems around them.

It was this same irrelevance that so alienated the young rebels in the sixties. They saw some Black preachers and some white ministers follow Martin Luther King in demonstrations against segregation. But these were the minority. Conservative congregations ousted young ministers who vocally supported King. The vast majority of church leaders pretended it was not happening. And, when King turned against the war and began relating both the war and segregation to economic issues such as the plight of the garbage collectors in Memphis, the religious community grew even more embarrassed and what support King had enjoyed began drying up.

My own split with the church had come long before the sixties and was over a more personal matter—masturbation. The Catholic priests that heard confessions in my youth were especially rough on that sin. I later decided that this was due to the fact that this was the one sin that they themselves were exposed to on a daily basis if they were taking their vows of celibacy seriously. Jesuit priests that came by periodically were even worse. They would get excited and rant and rave young adolescents like me who had no sexual outlet except the pleasure they could get from self-stimulation. Plagued by an enormous sexual drive inherited from my French Canadian ancestors, the issue bothered me enormously. I still believed most of what I had learned in Sunday school and was eager to please the church. Because I was brighter than average and had taken Latin, I was considered altar boy material. I even entertained thoughts of eventually becoming a priest. Masturbation was my first great problem with church teachings. Ultimately, I saw it as a choice between masturbation and salvation, and, naturally, being the red-blooded French Canadian that I was, I chose masturbation and have rarely darkened the door of a Catholic church since.

That physically based separation from the church was buttressed as the years went by with others garnered from history and science and by the time I left college I was a devout atheist. The sixties caused me to reevaluate some of my feelings, for while I learned much about the role of the church in human history from Marxist professors, I also saw the important role spiritual leaders like King and Ghandi played on the political scene. Stuck in Arkansas at the end of the sixties, I began a study of agricultural communities in the state and became impressed with the role churches played in giving the community a sense of direction and spiritual coherence. Their influence to be sure was authoritarian, brooked no opposition, was discriminatory and segregationist—yet, it still embodied some of the best instincts of the people in the community and it ameliorated some of the worst features of rural life providing some music, some solace for the grieving, and some meaning in an otherwise meaningless existence. Without the churches, there was no social life and no outlet for the better instincts of rural Arkansans. To that extent it made life better and one of the sadder effects of the growth of agribusiness was to destroy the basis of many of these communities and close the churches. As people piled up in the cities, the churches lost their influence and no longer were able to moderate many of the excesses that they were able to control in rural areas where family, church, and school were closely related and spoke with unity to guide the wayward youth and protect community members from sin. Also, about this time, I became involved with the Unitarian Church through the church's singles group. This church was different from any of the others I had come in contact with. It had preachers but no doctrine. It tolerated all manner of divergent beliefs. The only requirement seemed to be a token payment and the ability to be tolerant of others. In return one received all of the social amenities of a normal church with none of the guilt creating deficiencies. That, to me, seemed too good a bargain to pass up.

Yet, while I was pleased with Unitarian social life, I was not happy with the lack of community involvement that it exhibited. Most Little Rock Unitarians were content with their lives and were not willing to rock the boat. Hence, it had grown into a rather narrow enclave for like-minded, white, upper middle-class types who were usually well educated.

While the directives, such as they were, from the National Unitarian Church recommended vigorous social action, the local church, afraid of the conservative community in which it existed, was not very active. Rising to a position on the Board of Directors, I took it upon myself to change all that. Needless to say, about all I accomplished was to make the rest of the Board members, with the exception of one loyal ally, very angry at me, and, ultimately to make me even angrier at them. I was making them feel guilty—which is the worst thing you can do to a Unitarian since most of them have Baptist or Catholic pasts and they react violently to any evidence of a return to those awful feelings of guilt experienced so long ago. I quit the Board and would have quit the church had there been any place else to go.

At any rate, I have never stopped wishing there were some other church that was able to exert the influence on the community that those early churches in the small rural settings had. Only this time it would be a church that Marx could be proud of—one that acted in the community out of love as it created independently thinking, loving, young people used to arriving at their own decisions and acting upon them. People able to act out of unconditional love for others as they acted out of love for themselves and those closest to them.

Chapter Ten

Depression and the Bureaucrat
Shuffling Paper in the Age of Clinton

Literary people have long been fascinated with the bureaucratic phenomenon. Russian literature in particular has been rich in the critical treatment of bureaucrats—Gogol, Chekhov, Dostoevski have all reveled in belittling these easy targets for literary venom. Dickens, Thackeray, and Graham Greene have had similar sport with the British bureaucracy. American writers, however, have not been so fascinated with the problem. Most of them have preferred some variety of the frontier macho theme; man fights nature, the sea, the wild, poverty or drink. When the bureaucrat appears, he is only there to act as a prop for stronger forces and people arrayed against him as in the *Day of the Locust* or in Dreiser's *Sister Carrie*. Sinclair Lewis always threw in a few bankers to illustrate the cultural poverty of small town Americana, but generally did not deal with the nature of the bureaucratic personality. By and large Americans have tended to focus on the flash points in the economy rather than on the drudges that keep it going.

The Captains of industry—the Fords, Rockefellers and Carnegies—have received the lion's share of both the rewards and the publicity from the capitalist system. Tom Wolfe's recent foray on Wall Street, Bonfire of Vanities, captured another flashpoint, the broker—gambler who lives on the edge of either fortune or disaster. But that too is a long way from the drudges who hold the system together.

Americans seem not to enjoy the kind of caricature that is exhibited in British literature and on British television. We have, for example, no American equivalent of Monty Python and The Ministry of Funny Walks. At the other extreme, we have not developed an American Franz Kafka whose work carried the horror of the faceless bureaucracy to its pre-Nazi height in his novella, The Trial. American historians and economists have not done a whole lot better. This neglect may be because we have only relatively recently begun to endure what has long been a fact of life for these older countries—rule by Civil Servant.

But even in countries with the longest history of bureaucratic rule, Germany and Britain, a lot of ink has been spilled on the heroic struggles of the blue collar workers to organize and capture benefits for themselves and their families from industries determined to exploit their labor but not much has been done to illustrate the lives of the millions of clerks who organized the paper prisons that eventually enmeshed even the most heroic efforts of the workers to liberate themselves. Eventually, the clerk who understood the company pension plan came to lead most unions and he could only relate to the company clerk who handled the extraction of dues from the workers. The Jimmy Hoffas and John L. Lewises all faded into oblivion—what American on the street today can name three contemporary union heads? The faceless, nameless nerd with his plastic penholder tucked in his front pocket now controls billions in pension funds and more or less mechanically invests and divests as his computers dictate. The ability to organize a strike is rapidly becoming a lost art as major strikes become increasingly rare.

White-collar workers have long been noted for their unwillingness to join unions. Even in Britain and Germany where unionization is much more accepted than in America, only a small minority of these workers was organized. And, when they were, the white-collar unions were noted for timidity in approaching labor problems and conservative in their politics. In England, White-collar unions have consistently withheld support from the Labour Party and in America they have supported Republican candidates.

The reason for these right wing attitudes on the part of white-collar workers has a lot to do with status. As George Bernard Shaw put it fifty years ago, "the clerks have tall hats and hymnbooks and keep up the social tone by refusing to associate on equal terms with anybody." The first national union of clerks in Great Britain was organized on the premise that it would prevent the status of clerks from being lowered. White-collar work always paid less than skilled manual labor, but the clerks labored in the same building with the bosses and some of their attitudes rubbed off. And, since clerical work attracted those with good minds, weak bodies and made no demands on strength or courage, clerical ranks were soon filled with men who fit that description. Long apprenticeships and competitive examinations weeded out those who were either stupid or rebellious. It was, in its way, the job training equivalent of swaddling directed towards the development of wimps and nerds. Rewards were small but dependable, deferred gratification was rewarded with insured survival, and loyalty to the firm was the only real requirement beyond a modicum of skill. Status was primarily achieved by not getting dirty and by proximity to the bosses. Such training removed remaining spirit in the clerk at the same time continuous confinement to a desk soon eroded his physical strength. Correct employment attitudes were fostered by the bosses who rewarded bootlicking behavior. Clerks who demonstrated the right attitudes were given job security even in times of strikes. Promotions were slow but usually predictable. One waited until death and retirement offered opportunity for upward mobility. If one waited long enough and received enough education enroute, the clerk might become a boss—bureaucrat; a significant step for the lowly clerk. Frequently, second generation clerks became engineers and speeded up the process, sometimes leapfrogging into managerial positions over clerks who had served loyally for years causing great resentment. In the late nineteenth century, the ranks of clerks were swelled by women. One of the sadder, more morbid aspects of the introduction of women clerks into the workplace was the concomitant decrease in the opportunity for upward mobility that went with these jobs now reserved for females more or less for life—provided health and good attitudes were maintained. Women were expected to stay in their designated slot for the duration of their working life. Both World Wars accelerated the process. This dilution of the male ranks, made it even harder for remaining male clerks to maintain status and wages. It also made clerical unions much harder to organize, a problem that continues to the present day where female clerks remain unorganized, underpaid, and subject to all manner of exploitation. Males have generally left the lower levels of clerkdom to females and have taken over supervisory tasks; lower management positions, and migrated to sales and service jobs. None-the-less the clerk mentality remains even as male clerks rose into the middle classes.

As E.P. Thompson so brilliantly pointed out twenty years ago in his classic, *The Origins of the British Working Class*, The Protestant ethic was brought to the working classes and eagerly seized by clerks in the early nineteenth century as a cultural buttress to their efforts to rise above their working class heritage. Sexual and emotional deprivation combined with church approved concepts of self-denial and deferred gratification all worked to produce the sexually sublimated super clerk so mocked in the literature of the era. Schoolteachers, preachers, and career soldiers also exhibited these traits that had worked so well for their middle class masters. These traits indeed became the keys to economic advancement popularized by the major religious and self-improvement tracts of the period. Children were raised to be insecure, fearful, guilty and, above all, obedient to authority whether parental, state or church. As Freud pointed out years ago, "The capacity for independent judgment begins only when the individual begins to question parental authority." The combined forces of all the major institutions in society were devoted to preventing such questioning from ever arising. Alice Miller's work on German child training methods demonstrates through extensive quotes from German manuals the emphasis placed on procuring obedience through the use of psychological and physical terror. The question is not how such methods produced a generation of silent Germans and enough Eichmanns to supply the bureaucratic needs of the Nazi state, but how in the face of such totalitarianism numerous individuals managed to maintain their autonomy. The mistake Americans have made is to assume that this is just a German problem rather than one which all major industrial societies face. As long as these attitudes of self-denial, company loyalty, complete obedience, and acquiescence to authority were confined to lowly clerks, not much damage was done. Once, however, bureaucratic ranks began to swell with these individuals and they rose into positions of increasing importance, their dead weight began to become increasingly noticeable. Schools of engineering cranked out technicians with the minds of clerks. Deprived of the liberal arts training that might have broadened their perspectives and given them sufficient moral autonomy to make independent judgments when faced with moral issues on the job, they became powerful yes men for whoever gained control of the levers of power.

John Kenneth Galbraith was one of the first to note the

takeover of industry and government by bureaucrats in his book the New Industrial Age. He referred to them as "technocrats" and made much of the fact that Russian and American technocrats were becoming like interchangeable parts and it mattered little whether the industry was socialist and run by the government or capitalist and run by the market place—the decisions facing the technocrats were similar and so were the talents required. Galbraith's thesis was essentially correct—there is virtually no difference between the Russian and American technician. However, since Galbraith was trained at Harvard during the cold war, his education in Russian literature was neglected so he failed completely when it came to tallying up the results in cultural differences in the bureaucracies of the two countries; Gogol and Checkov could have told him what was wrong with his analysis; mainly, he forgot to factor in the extent to which history, conditioning, and the political system prevented the Soviet bureaucrats from utilizing their technical skills in the service of production—the much more brutal conditioning of the Soviet child from swaddling as a babe to political scrutiny from peers and ever present KGB police as an adult which went into the production of the timid, obedient, self-denying Soviet apparatchnik. From his position as the leader of the opposition to the worldwide growth of Stalinist influence, Trotsky was the first to bring attention to this ominous factor in the Stalinist system in a series of attacks from abroad, which described the nature of the new managers Stalin was placing in key positions within the Soviet system. Loyalty to Stalin both at home and in Communist Parties overseas took precedence to all other considerations. The needs of the economic system became secondary to this fundamental law of survival within the Communist system.

    Their American bureaucratic counterparts were not nearly so constricted in their efforts to apply the technical skills they had learned. Loyalty to the firm usually involved the search for greater efficiency to insure greater profits. Both systems exploited workers and were oblivious to environmental concerns. American managers suffered from other constrictions such as shareholders demands that led to the production of shoddy goods for short-term profits and the inability to invest sufficiently in research and innovation again because immediate profits were demanded by shareholders. But these inadequacies were nothing compared to the bureaucratic insanities placed on their Soviet counterparts who were required to meet political goals that had no relationship to economic reality and were forbidden by their political bosses from revealing that reality. Leaders were removed and dispatched to death or concentration camps by Stalin as his political whim or paranoia dictated. On the eve of WWII, for example, Stalin decimated the upper ranks of the Soviet military because of rumored disloyalty. Hence, when the war came, the Soviets were led by new and inexperienced, but politically correct military leaders. Rule by terror kept the bureaucracy in a continuous state of fear and insecurity and it was productive to the extent that vast feats of public construction—dams, roads and factories—the superstructure of an industrial state was quickly erected. Soviet bureaucrats, like the Nazi bureaucrats who ran the concentration camps were required to maintain silence under threat and they did so even after the threat was removed with the death of Hitler and Stalin. This silence-of-the-clerk seems to be universal. In the U.S., for example, there are no known cases of the retired managers of General Dynamics or any of the other large companies that have been found guilty of gross stealing in their war materials contracts with the government ever voluntarily coming clean. Clerks and petty bureaucrats within these companies rarely become whistle—blowers. This profound lack of conscious and dedicated loyalty to criminal institutions is perhaps the most frightening and virtually unstudied phenomenon of our time. Our only clear presentation of it has been in cases like the Eichmann trials in Jerusalem and Nurembourg trials following WWII. Of these, the Eichmann trial was the most revealing since Eichmann was more of a bureaucrat than a military man. It is said that Eichmann was so dependent on orders given from above that he would not defecate when seated on the toilet until permission was given. The famed Eichmann defense, that he was only following orders, was universally condemned in theory but it is also still universally practiced by German companies who have sold poison gas to little Hitlers like Saddam Hussein and Omar Kaddafy and unloaded toxic waste on the people of Albania without any protest from the bureaucrats within the guilty companies. It is fair to say that the Eichmann plea is still the defense of choice for bureaucrats who commit known evil every day.

What does it do to one's self esteem to knowingly do evil every day? Apparently it depends on how good the individual is at psychic numbing or what is a variation of the same thing, psychic splitting. In the first, the individual merely reduces all emotional reactions to the minimum required for continued functioning, one lives without responding emotionally to stimulus—swaddling children forces them to do this by enveloping them and forcing them through a period of sensory deprivation, which both dulls their senses and kills their spirit—a widespread child raising practice in both Germany and the Soviet Union that goes a long way towards explaining why those countries were able to endure Hitler and Stalin and have pioneered in the development of emotionless, mindless bureaucrats.

Psychic splitting involves the ability to shut down parts of one's personality; to do a job that is unrewarding or even evil and then go home to be a loving parent and husband. Protestantism encouraged this splitting through its denial of sexuality in the home. Since sex was unavailable in the home, the good German and British family man found his sex in the streets. What was forbidden in one area was permitted in the other. So also with work. Protestant countries tossed out the old Catholic guidelines for fair prices and just wages, thus separating the business world from the church. Eichmann was said to have developed this skill to a fine art. Helped by his ability to convince himself of his complete lack of responsibility for what happened on the job, he was able to see himself as a loving father and good citizen. Sometimes psychic splitting works in reverse as when those in the helping professions work long and diligently to solve the problems of those under their care while neglecting their own families, or a politician may be noted for his enlightened views on peace and civil rights but may treat his staff and his family with arrogant disregard.

Families, school systems, and churches may foster either authoritarian or democratic personalities depending on the extent to which they nourish the ability to make independent judgments, foster free expression, and provide opportunity for choice. Alice Miller has dramatically and poignantly portrayed how the Eichmann personality was fostered by the German school system as it crushed all expression of individuality, killed the self esteem of the students and rigorously demanded complete obedience; hence buttressing the job begun by early swaddling. To an extent every country has followed the Russian and German system, although most have given up some of the worst features such as swaddling and have replaced the brutal enforcement of discipline with more subtle systems of reward and punishment. Miller has also described how this works for gifted children who are psychologically turned into the narcissistic victims of proud parents, forever parroting the conditioned values injected +during childhood and never developing the capacity for independent action. The Japanese seem to excel at this form of torture and the psychological results are beginning to appear as Japanese managers frequently suffer from burn out, depression, suicide and general malaise despite a burgeoning economy. The Japanese have accomplished an economic miracle at the cost of the mental health of a large proportion of its own population. It has tried to compensate for this sacrifice by introducing its people to increased consumer goods that has been the American answer to the same problem. There seems to no end to the evil otherwise humane people will indulge in if the evil is presented as part of a job for which they are given enough money to purchase goods valued by their peers. People will sell drugs, pimp for whores, train to be killers, abuse, confine and torture animals, sell useless goods to unsuspecting consumers and manipulate public opinion to support all manner of health destroying products merely to make enough money to consume these useless products. Such consumption they are told will bring them happiness, and they believe that in spite of mounting evidence that it is not now true if it ever was.

Most philosophers and psychologists have agreed that the components of human happiness largely revolve around the concept of self-esteem, the development of autonomy, and the ability to create meaning in one's own life and in one's relationships with others. Yet, while there is near universal agreement that these are the components of the good, healthy life, few organizations in contemporary life actually structure themselves in such a way as to promote these values. Families, schools and businesses are by-and-large run on an authoritarian basis on the German model. Here and there some experimental families, schools, and businesses crop up. These, however, are too few to significantly alter the predominant mode of authoritarian family, school, and business structure. The result, as Alice Miller and others have demonstrated, is the adult emerges as a prisoner of his childhood, an incomplete person with an underdeveloped superego limited in its application only to loyalty to the most immediate authority and incapable of making independent judgments.

My own experience was no different than that of most Americans. My mother was a fairly typical, hard-working housewife struggling to feed six children in the middle of the Great Depression. There was not much love left in her by the time I arrived. We were taught to express no emotions, make no demands, and do what we were told by school and church. Mostly my brothers and sister did what they were told and have gone on to take relatively secure jobs in school or industrial bureaucracies. They have all been efficient clerks in the service of the systems in which they were placed—one helped make jet engines, another taught Junior High students to make things out of wood, another ran a mill that turned out lumber for houses for rich people, and my sister kept the books for the local gas company. They accomplished no great good but they did no great evil (with the possible exception of my brother who helped turn out jet engines for Pratt & Whitney—there is no telling what they were used for). I rebelled and spent most of my life attacking the system. Somewhere around the eighth grade, I had decided that the life being offered in return for compliance with the system was not for me. I was not conscious of actually making a choice so much as I felt impelled to rebel. I leaned towards the criminal life but I was never very good at it. I never had the really mean and ruthless instinct that is developed in the sociopathic family, Had the type of gangs that are commonplace in virtually every city today been in existence when I was coming up, I have no doubt that could have been induced into that lifestyle. As it was I just flirted with the gangs that did some of the criminal things that I had no appetite for.

Not knowing what else to do with my life, I drifted into the Air Force. Four years of drifting gave me an opportunity to enter college on the G.I. Bill where I discovered the good life in academia and student rebellion and I was hooked. I wandered around from college to college spreading the word about revolution until I was bumped off the academic gravy train in Arkansas and was forced to get a survival job in the state bureaucracy.

Now, like the rest of my family, I am trapped with the clerks.

Oh, I still talk and write about rebellion, but mostly I'm serving time like everyone else, deferring gratification until they pension me off and I am too old to handle much gratification. I often wonder if the state started burning Blacks and Jews, whether I would protest or, like Eichmann, follow orders to keep my paychecks coming. At first, I justified maintaining my bureaucratic position as a way of helping those groups outside the government become more aware of what was happening inside. I was a sort of mole. It is becoming increasingly more difficult to justify that position as the strength of the opposing groups outside government atrophy. After eight years as a clerk, I have come to adopt some of the features I described above, a lamentable concern with my pension, a horror of spending a poverty stricken old age, an increasingly conservative life style, and an inability to get excited about the old crusades that impelled me to protest in the streets, organize neighborhoods and write endless political tracts in the past. I go to weekly sessions with my shrink and occasionally take anti-depressants to ward off the bad feelings that come with doing less than what my superego thinks is necessary for complete mental health. The role my shrink plays as an agent of the system is to reduce the tension between what my rebellious nature thinks is justified action and what the system will allow in the way of change activity. The fact that this allows me to live without being destroyed by the system, compensates to some extent for the reduction in self esteem that comes with not doing what my analysis of the world in which I live tells me should be done. The drugs help, also. This is, in a way, a slightly healthier variation of psychic numbing. Since, however, it is done from a heightened awareness of my own neurosis and how to live with it, it is far less depressing than the denial that used to be the dominant feature of my existence.

Most shrinks know that healthy relationships, increased self esteem, and the free expression of authentic emotion relieves depression. It certainly has been true for me. Having neglected intimate relationships in the past while I toyed with what passed for revolution in the sixties, I have been painfully learning how to relate to myself and others as a means to gain the sustenance necessary to maintain a modicum of mental health. I hope to build from that base to include a wider spectrum of society within my area of concern while maintaining the security of a steady job—to develop a conscious that fits my ability to give, to continue as a change agent without destroying myself in the process. I'm still not sure that it is possible to hold down a government job and maintain self esteem, but economically I don't have a lot of choice.

Meanwhile, I look around at my fellow employees and see Eichmanns every where. My closest ally and fellow supporter of liberal causes, recently sold out and went to work for the state's worst polluter—since this is a pollution control agency, what he did is the moral equivalent of a Defense Department administrator going to work for a war contractor. The younger the employee, the more likely such a sellout will occur. The turnover rate for engineers is especially notable—most stay with the agency only long enough to learn the regulations at government expense and then go on to more lucrative jobs in private industry. My closest friend, a one-time fairly militant environmentalist has become a legal mouthpiece for polluting industries. Environmental protest groups that I once helped develop and tried to breath life in have withered by the wayside and died. Many of those remaining have become pitiful laughing stocks with virtually no credibility with the public or anyone. This may be only a local phenomenon. Nationwide, the environmental movement seems to be growing, but that growth has not affected the state of Arkansas nor has it affected the local pollution control agency.

The Director of that agency is an ex-auto parts salesman with no credentials as an environmentalist who owes his job to the fact that he once helped our current president win an election. His primary attribute is that he gets along well with industry. The enforcement branch of the agency is completely demoralized as they see their work developing cases against polluters being wasted through behind the scenes compromises worked out for the benefit of the polluter.

Worst of all is the silence. The denial of reality has become a way of life for most bureaucrats. On rare occasions and then in whispers, groups of disgruntled employees voice dismay. No one confronts; no one challenges. The price for moral integrity is too high. Job loss is a good possibility for those who do not conform to the recommended attitude of benign neglect. Promotion is given to those who go along and pay homage to those with power. The price for survival under those conditions is to allow a great deal of psychic damage or a profound lowering of self-esteem. As we have seen in the Eichmann case, it is possible for a bureaucrat to engage in either psychic numbing so that he is not affected by the corruption around him or he may engage in psychic splitting—split his personality so that he is an honorable family man and community citizen while he commits all sorts of near criminal actions at his job.

It is this training in psychic adjustment that allows the bureaucrat/technocrat to make the adjustment to consulting work where his talents go for hire or to straight industrial work where he is paid to represent industry directly (why the selling of technical skills for immoral purposes is not considered as morally reprehensible as the sale of one's body for sexual purposes has always been a mystery to me).

In either case, he becomes an "indentured savant", the technology skilled servant of industry bent on accumulating profit at the expense of the environment. In this capacity, the ex-bureaucrat takes one step further along the path of psychic corruption. Whereas in his old position he was only required to perform a certain amount of psychic numbing in order to overlook the destruction that was going on around him, the role of the indentured savant is to manipulate the data so that the results desired by the company are forthcoming. Usually this involves minimizing potential threats to the environment caused by the companies activities so that expenditures on environmental protection can be reduced to the minimum, hence, maximizing profit. The systems requires engineers to design minimal systems, construction teams to put them into operation, and lawyers to interpret the regulations that apply to the company's production. Outright violation of regulations is common since it usually cheaper to pay any fines that are forthcoming when caught than it is to properly meet environmental requirements. The legal indentured savant's main role is to intervene in the state regulatory system to get the fine reduced to the lowest level possible. The extent to which this is possible depends on the political power of the industry. Most larger industries have at least one legislator who does their bidding in return for campaign contributions. Pressure is usually placed directly on the Governor's Office which, in turn, applies pressure on the state agency to go easy on the guilty industry.

Industrial control of company towns is quite common in rural Arkansas. Since the town government controls waste water treatment facilities, deals are frequently worked out to disguise the true impact the company's discharge is having on the surrounding waters. In one case, the town of Berryville submitted samples taken on weekends when the local Tyson-owned, chicken-processing plant was closed, thereby disguising the normal impact the plant would have on the town's discharge. Such town's are so eager to have the jobs provided by the company, they are willing to go to any length to make them happy. The company, in turn, encourages employees to be active in all forms of local government so that company interests are well represented. With the able use of indentured savants, sympathetic politicians, and psychically-numbed bureaucrats, industries generally get their way at all levels of government.

In this struggle, environmentalists operate at an enormous disadvantage. Generally, the environmentalists come from the local community and are untrained victims of the industry's polluting practices. They usually labor under the impression that as taxpayers they are entitled to a fair hearing before the state agency charged with environmental enforcement. And, they are heard, but once caught in the maze of regulations, the normal citizen is helpless against the teams of well-paid indentured savants who work for the company. He usually shakes his head in despair and tucks his tail between his legs and runs. On occasion, the environmental atrocity will be so great as to attract the attention of national environmental groups such as Greenpeace. If so, their support can benefit the local victims. But it also can hurt as the cry of outside agitators, radicals, etc., is brought to bear on the proceedings. Even with the help of Greenpeace the environmentalists are still usually no match for the highly trained indentured savants. The clearest example of this situation in Arkansas was the with the efforts to halt the burning of dioxin at the site of the Vertac pesticide plant in Jacksonville. Local leadership opposed to the burning inside the city limits was led by a group of residents, largely women, who had been involved in the struggle to halt pollution in and around the site for years. Most of them had friends or relatives with various ailments they blamed on living near the plant which had produced a number of pesticides including the mixture of 2,4-D and 2,4,5-T which was known as agent orange and had been used in Vietnam. By the time the site gained notoriety enough to attract the attention of Greenpeace, most of the work on cleanup had been completed except for the disposal of over a thousand barrels of dioxin contaminated waste. The decision to burn the waste was considered the most acceptable alternative by both EPA and the local state agency. The citizens by this time were experienced in the ways of psychically-numbed bureaucrats and no longer trusted their assurances that it would be done safely without any substantial impact on the environment. But, in spite of help from Greenpeace, their protests were substantially ignored and the burning continued.

There is no way of knowing at this point who was right, the pro ar anti-burners. The science of burning dioxin is relatively new and it may go either way. The point to be stressed here is that the environmentalist were no match for the combined state and federal bureaucracies and the company savants. They were rolled over and largely ignored; considered nothing more than an irritant and an unpleasant distraction that reminded the bureaucrats that not everyone was as numb as they were and that the human spirit was still alive although not very well organized.

The other point that was clearly demonstrated by the Jacksonville case is how difficult it is to get the government to gather evidence which would indicate how severely the town had been impacted by the plant's production. Health studies were late in coming and barely adequate. Dioxin blood levels were measured only after production had been ceased and most of the worst excesses of the plant cleaned up and the majority of the affected population long gone. No effort was made to find and test those who were most likely to have been affected. And, dioxin was only the most toxic of the chemicals that were involved in pesticide production. Many of the other dangerous contaminants used by the company were more mobile than dioxin and hence more likely to appear in ground and surface waters were largely ignored.

The focus of public attention on this one deadly chemical was partly responsible for the lack of public inquiry about other problems, but surely the bureaucrats and savants knew better than to focus exclusively on dioxin. Yet, to a man, they kept silent (except, of course, for my own efforts—I wrote a memo discussing the other chemicals and the extent to which they had been released into the groundwater under the plant and requesting more testing in areas beyond the plant site). The memo was ordered picked up and destroyed). These were people who in theory were charged with defending the public interest, yet they knew their real job was to minimize costs, reduce damage estimates, and keep the public in the dark about the real nature of the environmental crisis. This same bureaucratic response can be seen in the handling of most other environmental problems. For example, dioxin was found in the fish below most of the state's major paper plants in the mid 1980's. This information was not brought to public attention for more than year after the fish were analyzed. The industry was alerted first and its big guns immediately hired savants to prove that dioxin was harmless and that the company discharges were also harmless. Greenpeace, since it was already in the state, got involved and again was ignored. The issue now has become; How much dioxin (notice again that the presence of other chemicals is being ignored) will the plants be allowed to discharge into the waters of the state. Bowing to industry pressure the state issued standards which were a hundred times higher than the recommended EPA limits for drinking water. The state claims that the limit applies to the discharge before it enters the water where it will be diluted to acceptable amounts. The environmentalists claim that such mixing cannot be guaranteed. The issue is not yet resolved, but if history is any guide, it is fairly certain the environmentalists will lose.

The state's largest water problem, however, does not involve anything so dramatic as dioxin, but plain, old salt. Wherever there is oil production and irrigated agriculture salt usually becomes a problem. Salt water is brought up mixed with oil from far below the earth's surface. Disposing of the unwanted saltwater then becomes a large problem. At one time it was merely dumped in the nearest creek where it killed fish and vegetation. That still happens in Arkansas, although it is now illegal. It is supposed to be held in tanks and overflow pits until it can be pumped back underground. The problem comes in two places; the integrity of the pits and how far below the ground the saltwater is pumped. Often the pits are merely dug in sand and allowed to leak their contents into the groundwater below them or to seep into nearby creeks. Injection wells are not given the same care as oil production wells and often the saltwater is not pumped as far down as it should be for safe disposal. As a result formations directly below drinking water supplies have been overloaded and are under dangerously high pressure which could allow their contents to migrate upward through cracks, fractures and old, well bores.

Many public water supplies (over twenty were above the 100 milligram per liter marker where the Health Department flags the water supply as a warning to those on limited salt diets and domestic wells in oil production areas now show some impact from salt. The same is true of rural community supplies in intensive irrigated row-crop production areas. Here the salt comes from residues left behind as the irrigation water evaporates. It then runs back into the creeks or is flushed downward into the water table by rainwater. To get pure water, the farmers dig ever deeper wells. Perched water directly beneath the fields may rise saturating plant roots or killing them through excessive salt. In places in Chicot and Desha Counties, vast acres of farmland are no longer useable because of the saltwater. Farmers there are increasingly turning to catfish production because the fish are more salt tolerant than plants and the salt also acts to hold down the growth of harmful bacteria. But, what is good for the fish is not good for humans, and, again, the bureaucratic response to the problem has been psychic-numbing. No studies on the health effects of communities whose water supplies are salty have been undertaken (although I formally requested them, I was informed the Health Department considered such studies to be too expensive).

No one knows how many domestic wells are too salty for safe human consumption. No state standards exist for sodium. The recommended EPA maximum for drinking water for those on a restricted sodium diet is 20 milligrams per liter. Practically every community in the eastern half of the state falls above that limit. Those who raise questions about these matters are ignored or shoved aside as I have been for eight years.

Since it is really difficult to fire a state employee, the usual procedure for dealing with those who do not indulge in the appropriate psychic numbing is to place them in positions of irrelevance and give them little or nothing to do. Hence, I am a planner for a program that has no real existence and involves little planning. My year's work can be completed in a few weeks. I get no promotions, no important assignments and write things like this on the job to keep my sanity and preserve a modicum of self esteem. To operate as a bureaucrat year after year and indulge in the required psychic numbing is sure to have profound costs in terms of lost self-esteem. As Alice Miller has demonstrated, "depression can be understood as a sign of the loss of self and consists of a denial of one's own reactions and feelings." And, "the opposite of depression is the freedom to experience spontaneous feelings." The bureaucrat not only denies his feelings, he also denies his humanity as he is forced to give up his compassion and his identity with the humans who will suffer from his willful suppression of the truth as he yields to pressure from the rich and powerful at the expense of the welfare of the majority. His psychic numbing reduces his superego or conscience to irrelevance—he is, then, killing his own mind. He can rationalize his behavior by saying he does so for the benefit of his wife and family, but do they really benefit if the result is they have a depressed husband-father who is not fully with them? And, is he likely to raise autonomous children capable of independent judgement and able to relate to others with compassion and understanding, or will they live out the lies they inherit from their father and their mother who is likely to become co-dependent on the lie? Will they like their parents substitute conspicuous consumption for integrity, independent judgement, an operational super ego/conscience? If one accepts the view that one's moral sense comes from a mixture of parental and societal views, that the superego incorporates the moral imperatives of one's family and society, and that the" capacity for independent judgment comes only with the questioning of parental authority," then the only hope is that the sons and daughters of bureaucrats will rebel, discard the values which brought their parents a lifetime of pyschic numbing, and initiate a new era based on autonomy, compassion, and free expression.

The End

About the Author

Ralph Desmarais writes and teaches in Little Rock, Arkansas. He has a Ph.D. from the University of Wisconsin—Madison and Bachelor's and Master's degrees from the University of New Hampshire—Durham. He has published three books, as well as over twenty articles covering a wide variety of psycho-socio-historical topics. He has lectured at numerous conferences including the American Historical Association, the Popular Culture Association, and on radio and television. His work has been supported by grants from the Rockefeller Foundation, the Arkansas Endowment for the Humanities, the Alcoa Foundation, and the Ozark Institute. He has twice won the Arkansas Literary Society Writing Nonfiction Contest. In addition to teaching, Ralph has worked as truck driver, social worker, counselor, bureaucrat, and volunteer fundraiser and organizer for a number of environmental and peace groups. He is currently involved in an ongoing struggle against urban sprawl in and around Little Rock.

Nonfiction titles from
Awe-Struck E-Books, Inc.
<www.awe-struck.net>

Fine electronic books in a variety of formats for your computer or hand-held device!

The Mind of a Terrorist Fundamentalist
by Stephen Morgan

The Anxiety Workbook
by Mary Ellen Popkin

Inside Out: A Volunteer Looks at Staying Motivated by Julie Eberhard Painter

And by new-age transcendentalist philosopher Laszlo Horvath:

Wilderness Alchemy

Masters of the Game

Observations from a Lookout
(also in print)

Visit Earthling-Press.com for the finest in paperbacks!
Romance, SF, fiction, nonfiction

<www.earthling-press.com>